MANNY PACQUIAO:

STORY BIGGER THAN BOXING

MANNY PACQUIAO: STORY BIGGER THAN BOXING

Published November 2009
Second Printing March 2010
Third Printing August 2010
October 2010

Cover Photo: Manny Pacquiao receiving his honorary doctorate degree on humanities from Southwestern University, Cebu, Philippines. Photo by Google Images.

Credits for other photos on interior pages: Marv Dumon, Google Images, Photobucket.com, BoxRec, International Boxing Hall of Fame, About.com, picsearch.com, Sports Illustrated and Memorabilia.com

Copyright Notice

Copyright © 2009-2013 is owned by Hermilando D Aberia

Pages from this book cannot be copied without prior written permission by Hermilando D Aberia. Hermilando D Aberia does not grant, except for personal and non-commercial use, any other rights in relation to use or distribution of this book. All rights are reserved. Permission to use the copyrighted materials of this book can be requested by writing to pacmandgoat@gmail.com or IM Institute, B15 L12, Kassel Kristina Heights, Tacloban City 6500 Philippines.

ISBN 1449596983
EAN-13 9781449596989

To

Auntie Sophie and Papa Nonoy of Hawaii, USA, and their families;

Onesimundo—my brother—and family;

Anesia, Anthia, Bernadith and Clara—my sisters—and families;

Gina—my wife;

Horasyo Roy and Hannah Kris—my kids.

TABLE OF CONTENTS

Foreword i

Part One: Dare To Dream, Dream to Dare 1
   Home Is the Hero 2
   The Way Of "The Pacman" 2
      Nothing But A Dream 4
      The Dream Comes To Life 5
      "Bruce Lee of Boxing" 13
      "Little Tiger From The Philippines" 16
      "Storm from the Pacific" 18

Part Two: More Than A Boxing Icon 20
   Way To The Top—A Replay 21
   Power of Will... 23
   Steroids? 26
      Pacquiao vs Mayweather 2 33

Part Three: The Greatest Of All Time 34
   Boxing Through The Years 35
      Amateur Boxing 36
      The Sanctioning Bodies of Professional Boxing 37
   All About Weight 44
   The All-Time Greats 47
      Fighters of the Decade 48
      The All-Time Great Lists 51
      The GOAT Debate 87
      Criteria For Ranking 88
      Notes On The Ratings 94
      Summary Of Ratings 95

Part Four: The Legend Grows 98
   Crusader in the Ring 100
   Who Can Stop The Pacman? 101

Foreword

Years ago, the Associated Press, ESPN, and The Ring Magazine, among many other media organizations, came up with their respective lists of who are the greatest boxers of all time. While they differed in their rankings from the second spot downwards, they had been unanimous in picking Sugar Ray Robinson as the greatest fighter of all time. One list picks Henry Armstrong at second, while the other puts Muhammad Ali in that place instead.

Results of a recent online poll supposedly participated in by more than half a million respondents further buttress the opinion that Robinson may indeed be the greatest boxer of all time, pound for pound. However, this time around, neither Armstrong nor Ali was to be found in second place. Instead, newcomer Manny Pacquiao came in second to Robinson, followed by Ali.

Boxing fans know, of course, that rankings and lists of all-time boxing greats are products of opinion. Thus ranking the world's greatest boxers (who competed in various eras and across weight divisions) is source of endless debate among boxing fans. This book joins this debate and wishes to argue its case with facts. The contention: Manny Pacquiao is even greater than Robinson.

In saying that Pacquiao has taken his place in boxing history as the greatest fighter who ever lived, pound for pound, we looked at the fight records of the world's greatest boxers. Although Pacquiao has done what no other fighter on planet Earth—living or dead—has achieved, we also look at his greatness in relation to what the other great fighters have achieved under their own unique conditions.

A critical part of our analysis of what these fighters had achieved is an evaluation of the quality of their respective opposition. It is in this context that Pacquiao has established himself as a top-level fighter, greater than Sugar Ray Robinson, Muhammad Ali, and Henry Armstrong, among others.

> Three things stand out from the core values that define the man. One is his inner drive. He needs no external push to envision and pursue his goals. Two, hard work. He puts effort into his craft like no one has probably ever done. And three, faith.

For example, 41 of Robinson's 200 fights were against opponents whose average career win percentage was less than 50 percent. In fights where these low-quality opponents were excluded, Robinson's winning rate goes down to 83.65, compared to his career win rate of 86.50. This pales in comparison to the resume of Pacquiao's opponents. Pacquiao has an average of 87 percent winning rate against high-quality opponents, compared to his career winning rate of 91 percent. Altogether—that is, including low-quality opponents—the average career win percentage of Robinson's opponents was 67, compared to Pacquiao's 72 percent.

This book also looks at several other evaluation or ranking criteria, such as how fighters coped with opponents deemed to be much heftier than they were.

Given what this book finds, it has become necessary to dig and verify facts on why Manny "The Pacman" Pacquiao is such a great boxer. In so doing, the reader is sure to find more of him. He is not only an exceptional athlete. He is, and precisely because of that, also a hard-to-duplicate person.

What makes Manny Pacquiao one-of-a-kind?

Three things stand out from the core values that define the man. One is his inner drive. He needs no external push to envision and pursue his goals. Two, hard work. He puts effort into his craft like no one has probably ever done. With hard work comes focus and determination. And three, the strength of his faith.

Give us one with those qualities and we give you an achiever—in boxing or in any field of human endeavor.

For millions who struggle in life and determined to come out of it a winner, the story of Manny Pacquiao should flare like a beacon.

Thus a good part of this book (first half of it) also tells The Pacman's story. The writing of the story attempts to pay homage not only to the man, but also to the kind of life he lives and the character that explains why he has succeeded in life. That story is about courage, determination and faith. It is a story that is bigger than boxing.

Hermilando Duque Aberia
Philippines
October 2010

Piety and Patriotism of Manny Pacquiao. Idolized as a boxing icon, fans know him not only by the way he fights, but also by his profession of Faith in God and allegiance to his country. Left photo, above, shows him up in prayer after a fight; right photo shows him celebrating victory by raising the Philippine flag. **Photos by Google Images.**

PART ONE: DARE TO DREAM, DREAM TO DARE

HOME IS THE HERO

Seventeen years ago, in 1994, 14-year-old Emmanuel Pacquiao, left his mother, Dionisia, and siblings in General Santos City, Mindanao, Philippines, for Manila, the country's capital city, to chase his dream of becoming a world boxing champion someday. Pacquiao then was not sure of filial support for his quest. So he slipped away from home without his family's knowing it. But he was sure of one thing: to return home as a world boxing champion.

Today, as he prepares for another record-breaking fight at the junior middleweight division (154 pounds) against Mexican and former world welterweight champion Antonio Margarito on November 13, 2010 at Dallas, Texas, USA, Pacquiao has been hailed as a hero and national treasure. He has returned not only as a world boxing champion. He has returned as the world's greatest boxer who ever lived, pound for pound. He has returned as a hero—not only for Mom Dionisia and family members, but also for the entire Philippines and sports fans worldwide.

THE WAY OF "THE PACMAN"

Pacquiao's ascent to the pinnacle of boxing throne went through the ultimate survival test ladder. No one in boxing history has done what he has accomplished. Among the world's professional boxers, both living and dead, he is the only one who had ever succeeded in winning world titles in 7 different weight divisions.

He embarked on a professional boxing career at 106 pounds and started to win world titles from 112 pounds all the way up to 147 pounds. He also succeeded—with aplomb—in beating the ten-time world champion and former light middleweight champion Oscar De La Hoya. In all, he has climbed 9 weight divisions (constituting an increase in weight of a total of 41 pounds). As this is written, Pacquiao remains on top of his game; and there exists the possibility that he might yet collect another world crown at a higher (junior or light middleweight) weight class. This will be against Margarito.

Beating weight handicaps at the higher divisions had been demonstrated by the likes of Bob Fitzsimmons—in 1897—and Roy Jones Jr—in relatively contemporary times. But their feats may not be as startling as pulling one off at the lighter divisions because, as Evander Holyfied puts it, at the heavier divisions a point is reached where one's punching power can be as potent as the other. Thus the case of Pacquiao is something else.

Al Bernstein, the multi-awarded sports broadcast-journalist, suggested in a September 2009 article that Pacquiao has reached a yet unheard of level of excellence, something that is beyond the usual even among the best of athletes. He said:

"Perhaps the most amazing part of all this is that Manny reinvented himself as a fighter when he

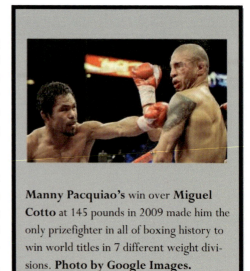

Manny Pacquiao's win over **Miguel Cotto** at 145 pounds in 2009 made him the only prizefighter in all of boxing history to win world titles in 7 different weight divisions. **Photo by Google Images.**

moved up in weight. He became a true boxer-puncher, using more movement, combination punching and widening his arsenal to include more right hooks. In his recent fights, he has been much more than the power punching, but sometimes one dimensional fighter he was in lower weight classes. He used power and toughness to get through wars of attrition. At the higher weights he has used guile, speed and, oh yes, still lots of power. I can't remember another fighter who has made such a transformation in his late 20's. It just isn't done. So, a unique place in history awaits Manny if he can find a way to beat Cotto. And what if he does that and then beats either Mosley or Mayweather Jr. after that? Well, let's cross that congratulatory bridge when we come to it. For now, let's contemplate one miracle at a time."

A couple of months after Bernstein wrote that article, Pacquiao did not only find a way to beat Cotto. He mauled Cotto before Referee Kenny Bayless halted the fight in the 12th. Some boxing analysis have attributed much of Pacquiao's success to the infinite amount of courage he brings to the ring when he fights. Bernstein brings up more dimensions to what Pacquiao does to boxing. He cites Pacquiao's skills—they keep on improving—power and toughness. Experts are almost one in saying that from a brawling and almost one-dimensional fighter that he was early in his career, Pacquiao has evolved into a tactical boxer-puncher.

This early we can add some more: hard work and faith in himself and in his God. Members of Team Pacquiao, particularly Chief Trainer Freddie Roach, have on many occasions in the past acknowledged that Pacquiao's work ethic is exceptional and is seldom seen in most other box-

Photo above (left) shows Heavyweight **Primo Carnera** and Flyweight **Frankie Genero**. Photo by **Boxrec.com**

AT HEAVYWEIGHT LEVEL, IT ALL COMES DOWN TO SKILL

At a certain weight, both of you hit hard and it comes down to skills; who's gonna hit who the most. But at a physical standpoint, a 5-pound and 10-pound difference is a major, major situation. When you're a heavyweight, it's whoever is gonna land that punch first, but it's gonna come down to skill. The person who's skilled is going to hit you more so they eventually going to knock you out too. When you both have about a 5 or 10-pound difference and you're a middleweight, the guy is just as quick. The one thing about me fighting the bigger guy at heavyweight is that I'm faster than them. If you're just a 10-pound difference in the lower weights, the speed is just about the same. If there ain't no difference in speed, then that person is hitting a lot harder and a lot stronger, how can you win? You have to be able to take that much force so it is a little different. That's why they made weight divisions because they knew it would be a big difference.

--**Evander Holyfield** in response to the question "You've fought guys that weighed 20 pounds more than you…How much weight actually makes a difference as far as the fight is concerned? by **Ben Thompson** of FightHype.com.

As a youngster, **Manny Pacquiao** went through physical and emotional hardships just to help his family survive. He says he understands what hunger means and knows how it feels when there is nothing to eat. However, these deprivations did not deter him from rising to live his dreams and eventually win the battles of life. In fact he would later admit that his low-life experiences, including losing a couple of fights early in his career, were the rock upon which his success as a prizefighter was built. His setbacks helped him develop the will power to withstand and overcome adversity. **Photo by Google Images.**

ers. And Roach has seen and trained lots of boxers, including the controversial heavyweight champion Mike Tyson.

Whenever Pacquiao is in training camp to prepare for a fight, the amount of effort, pain and sweat he puts into it is almost bottomless. His trainers would often restrain him to "take it easy." A typical day of his training regimen includes 30 minutes of road work in the morning and several hours of exercises (sit ups, push ups, skip rope, mitts, plyometrics, etc.) in the afternoon. Then he spars for several hours more on certain dates.

It is therefore hard to dismiss the point that hard work and preparation are keys to Pacquiao's success in boxing. Preparation (with an unquantifiable dose of help from Roach, among others), evidently, had done Pacquiao many things. It honed his skills (and for one who is naturally gifted in the first place), boosted his stamina, and raised his self-confidence level.

Early in his career, Pacquiao cited two reasons as to why his fights often ended the way they did (via KO). "They (his opponents) get tired," he said, "either from taking so many of my punches or from too much running away from me."

At this stage of his career, fights could end abruptly for quite the same reasons. The difference is that, as Bernstein suggested, the once best 1-2 puncher in the business has added to his ordnance more hooks and uppercuts, so people are bound to get tired even more easily. And, with Nike, "they can run," as Joe Louis warned Billy Conn, "but they can no longer hide."

Nothing But A Dream

The story of Manny Pacquiao is not only about the soaring to the height of greatness. It is also about the depths of misery—and how he showed the way to rise from it.

Early in life Manny Pacquiao had nothing—no money, no decent clothes, no formal education, not much food to eat. There were but a few whom he could call his family and friends. There was hardly someone he could turn to for counsel. He was so wretched that the possibility of him winning this big one day was simply unthinkable. No one (perhaps his Papa — who dumped the

Not quite a prizefighter yet, but **Manny Pacquiao** at 11 had already his eyes fixed on a future that may have been framed by his fists. **Photo by Marv Dumon.**

family for another — included) gave him a sporting chance in life—except maybe himself.

Today, Pacquiao is rich in many respects. His material assets could now be worth more than a billion of pesos. He has taken college courses. He has his own—and growing —family. The number of his relatives and friends has grown from a reluctant few to a cheering multitude, practically the size of an entire race—that of the Filipino and oriental race. And he now maintains hordes of expensive advisers.

Pacquiao fans could be rabid in their show of admiration for the man. It probably is not their fault. He simply is beyond the ordinary. His rise from the bottom to the top is phenomenal.

Let's recite, one more time, what he has done to be where he is today:

He started with nothing except the will to overcome adversity. He had nothing but a dream. He opened doors of opportunities for himself by deciding to become a boxing champion.

It was a decision backed by action. He toiled as he dreamed. He worked hard in the gym to hone his God-given talent in the sport. He put effort into his craft like no one ever did.

He tried to follow his star where others—boxing greats included—would not dare stick their neck out of their comfort shells. And, at 31, he has succeeded like no one ever did.

THE DREAM COMES TO LIFE

The story of Manny Pacquiao is not only a story about boxing. His story is also about hard work, focus and determination. His story is about courage. It is about heart. His story is about faith in himself and in his God.

Emmanuel Dapidran Pacquiao was born on December 17, 1978 in Kibawe, Bukidnon, Philippines, to parents Dionisia and Rosalio Pacquiao. He was the second child — and the eldest son — of the couple.

Bukidnon is one of the provinces located in Mindanao, the second largest island of the Philippines. The island is rich in natural endowments and is a major supplier of agricultural products to the rest of country. Most northern provinces, like Bukidnon, are heavy producers of grains, vegetables, fruits and livestock. The southern areas, on the other hand, like Davao and General Santos City, have boomed—aside from a robust agro-industrial-led economy—on the strength of their fishing sector, particularly their tuna industry.

The area, however, suffers from the widespread effects of poverty that debase the lives of a great majority of its inhabitants. It is divided and wracked by internal conflicts that for decades now have ignited intermittent bloody wars among Muslim militants, the armed forces of the country's national government, and even powerful clans. The nagging peace and order problem in Mindanao has been considered to be the single most debilitating cause of poverty in the area.

Being landless and not seeing many prospects in Bukidnon, and at the same time attracted by the livelihood opportunities offered by the tuna-rich and bustling General Santos City, the Pacquiao household would eventually pack up and leave Kibawe, move southward, and resettle in that city. It turned out to be a tough decision. While it was relatively easier to earn cash in the city (no matter how small the amounts), the change in surroundings did not bring dramatic changes to their lives.

If it was a struggle then, it was also a struggle now. Slowly growing in size and being the eldest son, family members expected Emmanuel to help generate some income for the family. And he sure did add muscle to tide the family over to the next day. He was also handy in several ways: by saving money that should have been spent on his clothes and shoes (he went to school with worn out clothing, unshod), by moving around the neighborhood (on foot, of course) with an assortment of merchandise like bread and ice water, or offer of services, like shining shoes.

In the meantime, the Pacquiao family grew with the arrival of two more siblings in as many years in GenSan. For being relatively newcomers in the neighborhood, the Pacquiaos initially existed as virtual outcasts. Friends were few, and those who called them relatives were even fewer. In such a condition, having more family members was a joy to be wished. It impacted on their already strained resources, however, and life for them soon turned from tough to harsh.

Rosalio decided to seek employment in a farm some hundred of kilometers west of General Santos City. He was driven, and in which the wife and children saw sound judgment, by promise of better livelihood opportunities.

But if relief from financial worries was forthcoming, more blows to the family was sure to beat it to the punch. After several months, the father started missing out on dates the family expected him to be around. The signs did not look good for the wife and children. True enough, it took only a few months more before they got to realize they have lost their man-of-the-house— the Philippines used to be a patriarchal society, after all—to somebody else's house. Rosalio, citing contentious marital differences,

Even as a youngster, **Manny Pacquiao** had developed a habit of dominating the opposition. His early flair for beak busting opened doors that led him to bigger breaks in boxing. **Photo by Marv Dumon.**

left General Santos City to live with another woman elsewhere—for good.

Dionisia and her children had to go through the emotional pain that soon rubbed in after sizing up the magnitude of their rejection. It was, for them, an added burden to a daily grind that wobbled under the weight of material want.

Gloom descended on the household but, happily, like a fairy tale, life went on for the deserted souls. At 13, Emmanuel left school so he could attend full-time to the needs of the family. He did more of the neighborhood vending, eventually branching out to other jobs—like hauling construction materials and doing laundry for a fee—odd enough for one so young. He rose to become the man of the house himself. The young Emmanuel—he who had nothing but a dream—would, in time, become Manny Pacquiao.

As the days went on and the daily struggles grew tougher, the will to survive and to come out successful emerged from the depths of Manny's young consciousness. He tried his hand on one of those boxing matches among boys meant to entertain the *peryahan* crowd during fiestas. He walloped opponents and forced them into submission, one after the other. He was an instant celebrity of sorts.

Having been rewarded with a token amount by the exhibition organizers, he went home with excitement, and readily remitted his earnings to his mother.

Each day Manny saw determination and courage in his mother. For a year now she was alone, mightily trying to bring 6 children up and for them to live at least nominally normal lives. Sometimes they found themselves comforting each other with jokes and laughter. Such moments were priceless and to be forever treasured, like having a Genie who lifted them up from the brink. They were a luxury, however, as reality kept forcing them to face the world, and their world was grim. It was time for Manny to tweak their fate and try to get some grip of their future. He was 14 when he decided to become not just a boxer, but a boxing champion. "If I become a champion," he told his mother and siblings, comforting them with this assurance, "we will have more money."

Lord of the prize ring—that was his dream.

He soon was working on the heavy bag he himself improvised. The masochists among peers engaged him in friendly matches—in streets, basketball courts, yards, etc. And it did not take long for them to find out that he could launch quite a fistic attack and embarrass an opponent.

His growing popularity among youngsters in the community led him to bigger things. He earned the respect and acquaintance of Abner

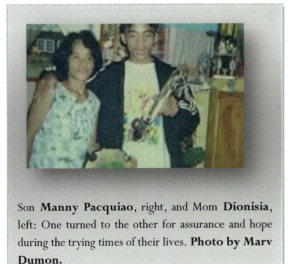

Son **Manny Pacquiao**, right, and Mom **Dionisia**, left: One turned to the other for assurance and hope during the trying times of their lives. **Photo by Marv Dumon.**

Cordero, a budding boxer himself. Abner's father, Dizon Cordero, was a boxing trainer (and who sometimes dabbled as manager) in General Santos City.

Everyday Manny walked a distance to make it a point he spent hours working on the bags, speed ball and ropes in Dizon's decrepit gym. The dream burned and starved for more ember inside; the words of encouragement and advice from the trainer became Manny's psychic nutrition.

An instant 2-member mutual admiration club came to life between Dizon and Manny. One saw a winner in the other. A few months later, an amateur boxing tournament held in Saranggani, a neighboring province, brought Manny and Dizon to their baptism of fire. Dizon entered Manny into the tournament and came out of it with passing grades. In fact, Manny topped it—zero loss in 5 bouts.

More ring action followed in the succeeding weeks. Dizon pitted Manny in 30 or so local "exhibition" bouts, winning most of them, with Manny earning an average of US$ 10 per bout. It was a windfall for him at the time. But Dizon conceded that bigger things awaited Manny in a bigger boxing arena, one that he could not find in Mindanao.

Barely 14 but loaded with dreams of a bright future in boxing, and equipped with nothing more than Dizon's counsel and a few pesos, he packed whatever scanty personal belongings he had, left his GenSan home, and sailed away for Manila in Northern Philippines.

Dionisia and the rest of her children would later know about the daring flight only through a note Manny left. The message vowed filial commitment, and a promise that he will return in glory. "Pray for my success, Ma," it said.

With Dizon's referral and help from a maternal cousin who had made Manila his home, Manny was able to seek out Polding Correa, who eventually brought him to the operators of L & M Gym in Sampaloc, an old district of Manila. But while he got to wear gloves and the equipment he needed for training (the place was open practically to everybody), fighting as a professional and thereby begin to earn a living from it was still a problem. For one, government sports regulatory guidelines had imposed, among other things, the minimum age limit—18—on boxers applying for a professional license. He was only 15. He was out, for the moment.

His dreams crash landed on planet Earth and, no matter how manfully he tried it, he could not hide his disappointment as visions of the long wait stared at him.

For another, nobody could really commit to help manage his unborn boxing career—yet.

Apart from his career vision, there were immediate concerns to attend to. Due to his ineligi-

Manny Pacquiao becomes a study in focus and determination as he sweats it out using improvised training facilities. **Photo by Marv Dumon.**

bility for a job in the prize ring, survival for Manny Pacquiao became another struggle in Manila like it was anywhere else that he had been. And so, to keep body and soul together, he took all sorts of odd jobs—mostly in construction sites.

If a harsh life could create an unbreakable willpower in a boxer, then Pacquiao—unflinching in the middle of a storm—was surely headed to greatness. Early signs had shown he was getting there. For instance, he never lost sight on his commitment to boxing. As in Dizon's gym, he remained like an internal contraption of the L & M Gym.

During this time a weekly boxing show "Blow By Blow" was running at one of Manila's minor TV outlets with more or less nationwide coverage. The show aired recorded bouts, most of which held in Manila and nearby areas. The producers and commentators of the show included Mon Lainez (one of the owners of L & M Gym) to whom Pacquiao was ceded by Correa. Fight promoters and sponsors often linked with producers of the show for purposes of recording and airing the fights on TV. One such sponsor had organized a series of benefit bouts in Oriental Mindoro, one of two provinces in an island west of Luzon. Would Manny accept the offer of fighting in Mindoro?

Lainez, who, along with Lito Mondejar and Rod Nazario, eventually became Pacquiao's business managers, had seen Manny spar and work on the heavy bags. He was impressed with what he saw. The prospect of seeing Pacquiao in actual ring action was enticing.

With a handler in Lainez and company, Manny felt that a license might not be critical a requirement in a remote place like Mindoro as it was in Manila. He was therefore thrilled and elated to accept his first professional assignment.

He wrote what he felt on a bond paper, sealed it in an envelope and sent it by post to General Santos. The tone of excitement was unmistakable as he reminded his Mama and siblings several times to watch him fight on TV. Informed of when his ring debut would be aired, he emphasized the date: January 29, 1995. It was a Sunday. Being under-aged, the fight organizers also required parental consent from Pacquiao, and he asked his mother to send it—and quickly—to him.

Under normal conditions, the pre-fight routine would include, aside from the basic weigh in, medical check-up for fighters and presentation of the required licenses.

But fights of this kind were unusual in many respects. To meet the required minimum weight, Pacquiao stuffed his shorts and shoes with coins and small pieces of metal. He presented his mother's consent letter in place of a professional boxer's license.

His efforts at getting through the pro-fight regulations were just about the most thril-

Manny Pacquiao launched his professional boxing career at age 16 on Philippine television via the weekly boxing show "Blow by Blow." **Photo clip from You Tube.com.**

ling part of his pro debut. A curtain-raiser, the fight itself was not exciting. The opponent kept on either tying him up with hugs or dancing away since the middle of the first round until the bout ended in the fourth. But there was something in Manny, who was so thin he looked like Popeye's Olive, that made the show producers pick him as one of its regular performers. Pacquiao's dangling fists had served notice of their sting, and Edmund Ignacio, the opponent, acknowledged it by getting out of their reach.

Manny won his pro debut by decision. Back home, applause and glee reverberated from Pacquiao's neighbors (Dionisia went downtown to see his son on TV from an appliance store) as they watched his hands hoisted by the referee to proclaim him as the winner of the bout.

Pacquiao returned to Manila like a millionaire he felt he was. Who wouldn't? His first professional fee was worth 25 US dollars.

On Sundays that followed, more rounds of excitement and applause echoed from the neighborhood, which soon spread to the entire community, then the whole of GenSan, and eventually throughout the boxing constituency in the Philippine archipelago.

In the local dialect the word "Pacquiao" roughly means "to buy in bulk," or to get a work done "by lot" (which is recommended when the intent is to rush it), instead of by completing the pieces together one by one, or by getting paid on a daily basis (which normally accomplishes things at a slower rate). Thus Pacquiao, the rising TV star, evoked images of one who annihilated his opponents by lot, one after the other, in the quickest way possible.

After 10 Sundays of seeing him fight on TV, Filipino boxing fans have started to take glimpses of a future ring sensation in him. The show itself had enjoyed decent viewer ratings. Sponsorships poured in. Boxing venues burst to the rafters when a Manny Pacquiao was in the card. Politicians, always quick with ways that make people notice them, organized boxing events that featured him as main draw. He attracted quite a number of female fans and admirers as well. And while he wooed some of them, he was particularly interested in one Maria Geraldine Jamora, also called "Jinkee."

When watching sports-oriented TV shows, even outside of the now-famous "Blow By Blow," people would easily recognize boxing by Pacquiao when the fighter they saw was on constant attack, almost by cadence, that the crowd could cheer with the flow of his rhythmic bang bang. They could feel the rush of his adrenalin like it was their own, revving them up—one that ignited a bombshell of cardiac animation, electrifying the crowd itself—as Pacquiao hopped and hinged on his toes, chasing his prey, hips and shoulders set for the launch of his rapid 1-2 rifle shots. Gasps followed as the Pacquiao ammo exploded, hitting the target, the other guy sprawled on the canvass, and the referee waving his

Attracted to **Maria Geraldine "Jinkee" Jamora**, left, right at their first meeting in their late teens, **Manny Pacquiao** wooed her heart in a whirlwind of a courtship that did not go the distance. The two would eventually marry and now have 4 kids. **Photo by Google Images.**

hand to make the abbreviated outcome official.

"Another work by Pacquiao" fans would say after watching a sudden end to a fight. He was, to the crowd, a delight to watch, like an artwork in motion.

Pacquiao would produce 11 of such artworks in succession within the year of his joining the professional ranks. Somehow government officials had found a way to grant him his clearance as a full-fledged professional boxer. After all, going by his performance so far, it was hard for anyone to argue against his fitness as a professional boxer.

Then one bad night for Pacquiao and his fans came, as it sometimes happens even to the best of athletes. He faced Rustico Torrecampo, a dangerous opponent although less of a performer with an 11-4-4 win-loss-draw record, on February 9, 1996. In the third round of their fight, Torrecampo sneaked in a solid left to Pacquiao's jaw. In a flash, it flicked the lights out of Pacquiao.

"*Patay kang bata ka!*" ("Dead is the kid," street slang for one who has been hit by a shocking misfortune), a spectator blurted out.

When he came to, he found himself counted out. His corner man bodily lifted him up towards his corner. He looked fine, however, and in a few seconds he got up as if nothing happened. He shook his head and smiled sheepishly, the look of embarrassment written all over his face.

The partisan crowd that filled every inch of Mandaluyong City Gym, the boxing venue, stared in disbelief, silenced by the unexpected turn of events.

Then came the reactions. "He was kind of cocky out there," intoned Torrecampo after the fight.

"He is human, after all," remarked a dejected fan. It was amazing how people could see a superhero in such a greenhorn of a fighter as Pacquiao.

For the fallen "superhero," the dream—revived and in flame the past 12 months—crash landed once more. The psychological wreckage was as nasty as the physical pain he suffered. While the pain was gone in an hour, his bruised pride followed him even to his sleep. Will the road to my championship dream re-open? The doubts must have weighed heavily on him. He eventually skipped the gym routine and went back to construction work. Giving up on his championship dream seemed easy at this point.

"I felt I wanted to quit," he said in one media interview where he recalled the pain of suffering the first loss in his boxing career.

Down and Out. **Manny Pacquiao** crashed to the floor after he got hit by a single left shot from upset-conscious **Rustico Torrecampo** with barely 22 seconds into the 3rd round of their fight on February 9, 1996 at Mandaluyong City, Philippines. **Photo clip from YouTube.com.**

But if anything good could come out of a setback, it was that one got to regain his humility. The rest that put a man with a mission back on track followed. He recovered his capacity to look at things from a more realistic perspective—lots of bravado went into his dare of fighting without thorough preparation against Torrecampo (he came in 1 pound over the agreed weight limit and was penalized with heavier gloves). He realized there was no room for carelessness in his chosen job.

Pacquiao's handlers regrouped to re-assure themselves and the boxer. They looked at the future: Surely, a talent with such a promise could not be dashed, dismissed and consigned to obscurity by a solitary loss. What if—from the viewpoint of business—this unpredictable yet explosive fighter could become a cash mill someday? Would fight promoters fight among themselves just to have a grip of this guy? They charted a new path for Manny.

Two months later, Pacquiao was back in the ring. It was much like the way he started: a win by decision. The difference was he was now a 10-rounder.

From then on, it was back to signature boxing by Pacquiao. Eleven straight wins, 9 by knockout, 4 of the knock outs taking place in the first round. He was back on the saddle. The chase for the star was on.

Again.

At 19, he went to Thailand to contend for the WBC Flyweight belt owned by local favorite Chatchai Sasakul.

On fight night, December 4, 1998, Sasakul was clearly a crowd favorite. He had lost only once in his 31 bouts (to Yuri Arbachakov, whom he defeated in a rematch), with 24 of his wins all by stoppage. He had merited for himself a kind of national adulation that was reminiscent of the times when Khoasia Galaxy was king of the world's flyweights. And for a country that hooked its first Olympic Gold from boxing, Sasakul had become a folk hero.

But despite Sasakul's "home court" advantage, it was clear from the opening bell that Pacquiao was determined to bring the fight to the champion. He did not look awed one bit by Sasakul's fearsome record, leaping forward with 1-2 right-left straights in a fast-paced attack.

The champion countered effectively, however. He kept tagging Pacquiao with his own arsenal of shots, sometimes making it look like one was matador and the other was bull. Sasakul effectively adjusted to Pacquiao's unrelenting pressure, rolling his body to the left every time Pacquiao fires the first of a series of shots. It saved Sasakul from getting hit with quite a number of lefts—which appeared to have gener-

If something good could come out of a defeat, it is, in the case of **Manny Pacquiao,** the lesson that is learned. His loss to **Rustico Torrecampo** taught him the value of thorough preparation before each fight. **Photo by Marv Dumon.**

ated the most damaging effect on Sasakul—from Pacquiao.

By the sixth round, it looked like the relatively unknown challenger was not only shaming the popular champion in front of the home crowd, Pacquiao was also hurting Sasakul with power shots. And then pride—or whatever it is that compels one to hit back when hurt—must have forced Sasakul to abandon whatever boxing technique he mastered; he decided to answer fire with fire, toe-to-toe, in the center of the ring.

It did not look good for Sasakul. The matador turned bull and put himself at the same level as his quarry.

A Pacquiao left found Sasakul's chin and Sasakul staggered backwards. The crowd froze, probably sensing that a few more of that choice shot could end the fight.

The fight did end sooner than expected. In the eight round, a sledgehammer left from Pacquiao rocked Sasakul. Sasakul reeled backwards as he groped for the center of his body's gravity, barely succeeding to keep his balance. But Pacquiao was back in no time with yet another 1-2-3. Sasakul was visibly in dire condition as he retreated even farther. The attempted flight, however, failed him as the knees wobbled like a rubber stand, unable to carry him away from more harm. He managed to lean with his back on the ropes long enough to see that another Pacquiao left was coming. Defending with all his might, Sasakul moved his right glove slightly to the left in an effort to block the ignited missile. But the look of determination in his face turned to terror as the Pacquiao warhead arched gracefully to the left before it exploded right on his chin.

Sasakul crumpled to the canvass, face down. He struggled to get up as the referee's count up reached 7, only to slump back to the floor, head first, before rolling over until he finally settled with his back on the floor. Pacquiao knocked the champion out.

As the ring announcer officially declared the ending of the bout and proclaimed Pacquiao as the new WBC Flyweight Champion of the world, and as the referee raised his arms, Pacquiao glanced upwards, as if to acknowledge the clouds above him. He went to his corner, knelt down and covered his face with his gloves. Then jubilation from among the small Team Pacquiao members erupted. It was time to celebrate.

> *I see the opponents going down. But I did not see the punch that hit them.*
> --**Murad Muhammad**, after seeing the fight tapes of **Manny Pacquiao** for the first time

After 3 years of hunting, Manny Pacquiao collected his prize. The world championship was won. It was his moment. His dream has just come true.

"BRUCE LEE OF BOXING"

Manny Pacquiao's reign as flyweight champion did not last long—9 months—but enough for a baby to grow inside his mother's womb and eventually see the light of day. Manny and Jinkee had, by this time, got married and their first child, Jemuel, was born. In the meantime, on April 24, 1999, Manny defended his title against Mexico's Gabriel Mira, whom he defeated by TKO in the 4th round. Within 2 months Manny would again defend his crown for the second time against Midgoen Singsurat of Thailand, and should have been, by this time, in deep training for that defense. He was not. His being a father for the first time must have shown him other precious things in life apart from boxing.

When Manny did start his preparation for the Singsurat fight, his new-found celebrity status created problems not so much because it often took away his focus, but simply because the Filipino in him could not simply say no to anybody. He also had to cope with the needed adjustments at the home front, only to realize that some things were harder to knock down than a ring opponent. For one, Jinkee and Mother Dionesia—whose disappointment over Manny's early marriage was partly aggravated by a dashed personal wish for him to make it to the priesthood—were not in the best of terms. For another, too many fans, friends, relatives (hordes of them were coming forward from nowhere), and admirers (from the opposite sex) were competing for his attention.

Manny had a less than satisfactory work rate at the training camp. On the day before the fight, he was overweight by 1 pound. The WBC had no recourse but to strip him of his title even before a single punch could be thrown by either fighter.

On fight night, September 17, 1999, a visibly drained Manny Pacquiao faced Singsurat for a ring battle he could not win. It appeared from the outset he did not have the amount of energy or motivation he needed to overcome the challenge he was facing.

When the bell rang, Singsurat tagged Pacquiao at will. And as the fight progressed from one round to the next, its complexion remained unchanged. It was all Singsurat. In the third round, an out-of-shape Pacquiao grimaced as he absorbed more punishment from Singsurat's body attack.

The lopsided bout soon came to an end. Pacquiao lost by knock out. His belt was now wrapped around the challenger's waist.

"We have to be candid—we did not prepare thoroughly enough for this fight. And besides, the kid is growing up," Lainez explained to media as to why Pacquiao failed to make weight.

If lack of preparation and weight problems brought down Pacquiao in his loss against Torrecampo, they must have also did it to Pacquiao in his second defeat.

This was one more lesson-of-the-same- kind learned the expensive, and painful, way.

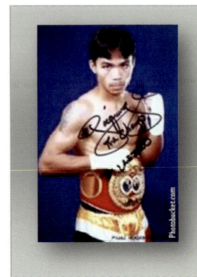

At 13, **Manny Pacquiao** had wanted to become a boxing champion. At 19, he won his first world title. By the time he turned 30, he already won 7 belts in as many weight divisions—something which no other boxer, living or dead, has accomplished. How he did it is a veritable how-to's of managing the blocks and humps of life, a study in the unbreakable spirit of one who is driven by a mission. **Photo by photobucket.com**

Pacquiao soon decided to move up in weight. In three months, he was back in the ring, fighting as a super bantamweight.

Invading the higher weight division seemed to be perfect for the 21-year-old Pacquiao. In his first fight as a super bantamweight, he knocked out Reynante Jamili in the second round. And from there he racked up 6 straight wins, all of them by knockout.

A close look at Pacquiao's last 6 opponents made it difficult for aficionados to ignore his potential as a great fighter. They were top-level opposition, having compiled an average winning rate of 86.7 percent (as compared, for example, to that of Sugar Ray Robinson, who had a career win percentage of 86.5). All 6 fights were 12-rounders; but they lasted only an average of 4.7 rounds.

As Dizon Cordero advised Pacquiao 6 years ago in General Santos City, Pacquiao's handlers felt that he needed a bigger arena in which his full potential could be harnessed to the limit.

Rod Nazario and company had in fact been shopping for fight promoters and trainers in America ever since Pacquiao became a world champion. Pacquiao's handlers felt America was the place to sell the exciting brand boxing he was capable of dishing out. The American boxing fans, after all, had the means and were willing to pay for boxing shows they liked. In short, America was where real money could be made.

In one episode of Pacquiao's career that years later would prove to be a masterstroke, he ended up being mentored by Freddie Roach. A former professional boxer himself who learned the ropes under the tutelage of the legendary Eddie Futch, Roach owned and operated Wild Card Gym, a boxing training facility in Los Angeles, USA.

Unfortunately for Pacquiao, however, it seemed no American fight promoter was interested in him. He was a nobody in America. If he was not an item, what business opportunity could he offer? The one or two who heard of Pacquiao knew he lost by knock out in his last title fight.

But before Team Pacquiao could gave up on its American dream, it found some sort of a breakthrough in initial talks with Murad Muhammad, an American promoter who toiled in the shadows of Don King and Top Rank's Bob Arum.

For Pacquiao's handlers, it helped that Murad had earlier been associated with some people in the Philippine boxing community. Murad was part of Muhammad Ali's team when the latter fought Joe Frazier for the third time in Manila in 1975.

> Some say he got guts. Others say he got class. Pacquiao says Pacquiao simply wants to make the fans happy.

Murad went over the Pacquiao tapes several times. He saw Pacquiao's opponents crashing to the floor. But he could hardly see the punch that knocked them down.

Murad said of Pacquiao: "He is like Bruce Lee."

Murad quickly went to work. Working on a fight card that would feature Oscar De La Hoya (who just severed promotional ties with Top Rank), he assembled the hawks he needed to beef up the undercard. He also called up his friends at HBO. But where Pacquiao was concerned, the network giant hesitated. Some of its big bosses apparently also got wind of Pacquiao as "the one who was knocked out in his last title fight." They doubted if Pacquiao was "entertainment" material. They thought he had little value insofar as boosting pay-per-view sales was concerned.

But Murad persisted. He dug deep into his stack of aces. He offered deals and haggled. He knew a gem was in his hands.

"LITTLE TIGER FROM THE PHILIPPINES"

In the meantime, over at South Africa, the HBO covered Hasim Rahman's gigantic upset knockout win over Lennox Lewis, who was then universally-recognized as the lineal heavyweight champion. The undercard of the Rahman-Lewis fight featured, among other bouts, another title fight at the super bantamweight division involving Lehnoholo Ledwaba, the champion.

Nicknamed "Hands of Stone," Ledwaba's resume did indicate the rise of a new Roberto Duran, having beaten all but one of his 30 opponents, most of them by knockout. A complete package of boxing entertainment, Ledwaba turned out to be a star of the night, prompting the HBO people to think aloud about prospects of showing Ledwaba to a bigger crowd.

And true enough, HBO did set up a fight for him in the United States.

Ledwaba's entry to big-time boxing was, well, big time. He was set to defend his title in the undercard of Oscar De La Hoya's bid for a record 5th world title in as many weight classes against Light Middleweight Champion Javier Castillejo. By that time, De La Hoya had already loomed as a pay-per-view behemoth. Practically the entire global boxing community would be around to watch Ledwaba perform.

But if Ledwaba was lucky to earn for himself a ticket to the mainstream of professional boxing, Pacquiao was even luckier. He was picked as a late replacement to contend for Ledwaba's title.

Pacquiao's "luck" did not go unnoticed in the eyes of boxing's partisan observers, however. Some fellow boxing promoters in the US, for example, kidded Murad about how he (Murad) succeeded in inserting Pacquiao to the De La Hoya-Castillejo under card. Sanctioned by the IBF, Murad was known to have close ties with its president, Marian Muhammad. Murad explained that Pacquiao, ranked number 7 by the IBF at the time, earned his shot at Ledwaba's title after the unavailability of the top six contenders in front of Pacquiao had been verified and confirmed.

Back to the Ledwaba-Pacquiao fight: it was in Las Vegas, USA, June 23, 2001. As the bout was about to start, the HBO commentators did mention that Pacquiao came to the fight on a two-week notice. What they did not say on air was that they brought Ledwaba from Africa to treat the American boxing crowd with a delighting display of boxing—courtesy of Ledwaba, and that whoever would materialize to challenge Ledwaba could be nothing more than prey for the African predator.

Such a perception quickly vanished as soon as the two fighters exchanged hostile leather. Pacquiao took one; he gave one dozen. If Ledwaba had quick hands and feet, Pacquiao had a quicker pair of both. If Ledwaba had stones in his hands, Pacquiao had bombs.

The Las Vegas crowd had seen both fighters only for the first time, but they sure were enjoying the work they were seeing. They roared in approval as Pacquiao pressed his attack. He whacked hard. He shot sharply. He was relentless. And he was fearless.

As Pacquiao approached his corner after the bell rang to end the second round, the crowd loudly applauded him. He acknowledged the gesture by raising his gloves, as if to thank them for appreciating his effort.

The Ledwaba-Pacquiao fight was meant to be an appetizer to the De La Hoya-Castillejo main dish, but the crowd looked like it was already full. Pacquiao was giving them their money's worth.

By the sixth round, Ledwaba must have felt too battered to think of any boxing science he knew. He brawled with his opponent. It was reckless and suicidal on his part. He did not finish the round in upright position.

Larry Merchant, HBO's main mike, remarked: "This is the first time I have heard about and seen Manny Pacquiao, but now that I have seen him, I want to see more of him."

Indeed it was a fight that moved the fans to ask for more of its kind. They would not be disappointed. Five successful title defenses by Manny of his title followed, all of them by knockout.

Media edged to know what else Pacquiao could offer to the fans. What's next for Manny? I want to fight Marco Antonio Barrera, he said.

Not a few would find, at that time, that the kid in Pacquiao was kidding. Barrera held no title, but he was hailed as the "People's Champ." He had beaten undefeated and marquee fighters that included Johnny Tapia, Erik Morales, and Prince Naseem Hamed, among others.

Not only was Pacquiao a relatively unknown fighter challenging a Boxing Hall of Fame shoo-in, he was also an untested super bantamweight pretender challenging a proven world-beater that lorded over the higher featherweight division.

But, on second thought, if his having devoured Ledwaba when organizers thought Ledwaba would eat him alive was any measure, then Pacquiao must have felt he deserved to be tested.

It turned out Pacquiao wanted to test his limits all the time. From the time he sailed away from General Santos City to Manila he knew nothing about, then his ring setbacks on account of complacency, and then to a second world title few people thought he was capable of winning, there emerged the essential outline of what drove the little man: he looked for the toughest challenge there was and dared to take it.

On November 11, 2003 Barrera and Pacquiao fought for recognition as Ring Magazine's top featherweight, along with the lofty

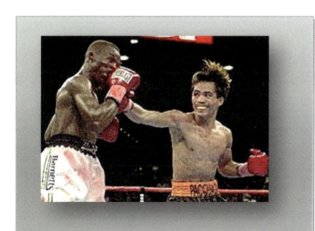

On June 23, 2001, **Manny Pacquiao**, a late replacement, challenged IBF Super Bantamweight Champion **Lhenohonolo Ledwaba** of South Africa for the latter's title in Las Vegas, USA. **Pacquiao** TKO'd **Ledwaba** in 6 rounds. Photo by Photobucket.com

mythical tag of "People's Champ" in Texas, USA. The odds were 5-1 in Barrera's favor, indicating the remoteness by which the fans gave Pacquiao any chance of upsetting Barrera.

It took only a couple of minutes before Pacquiao showed the fans that Barrera, not him, had no chance of winning the fight. Merchant could not believe what he saw in the ring. He had expected—like many others—a demolition; a demolition by Barrera of Pacquiao, not by Pacquiao of the great Mexican. He could not believe how Barrera got clawed by what he called "the little tiger from the Philippines."

The fight was over by the eleventh round. Barrera's corner rushed to his aid and save him from further damage. Merchant told his TV audience: "Manny Pacquiao has just shaken the boxing world."

"STORM FROM THE PACIFIC"

Adoring Filipino fans became a common sight wherever Manny Pacquiao went. He was a boxer; but the magnitude and meaning of his achievements, his overall mien, the attitude and the discipline that made him a winner all helped define who he was, and the glow of his light transcended the sport. Wracked by social, economic and political strife, his countrymen saw in him the face of a nation that badly needed a hero.

Pacquiao was up for exaltation by a grateful nation. He was on his way to super stardom.

Not so fast, however. He gored Juan Manuel Marquez in the first round of his next fight. But he failed to finish the Mexican. The judges ruled the fight a draw, although one of them would later admit he erred in his addition. At any rate, the broader boxing community remained divided in the verdict of who among the two was the superior fighter.

Pacquiao met Erik Morales in his next fight—ten months after the draw with Marquez—on March 19, 2005. It was Morales' turn to gore Pacquiao—literally this time. In the fourth round, a head butt which the referee ruled as accidental opened a nasty cut above Pacquiao's right eye. Blood flooded Pacquiao's face until the bout ended in the 12th round. Morales won by unanimous decision.

In that fight, the two warriors waged a contest that put on display the triumph of athletic excellence. Apart from that, Pacquiao showed not only his enormous courage in the middle of dire situations, but—as blood freely dripped from his cut—also his capacity to tolerate pain. That loss helped grow, rather than diminish, the stock of the Filipino.

Pacquiao and Morales went to war two more

Mexican **Marco Antonio Barrera**, left, looks for comforting signs from his corner in his November 15, 2003 fight against **Manny Pacquiao** in Texas, USA. **Pacquiao** dominated **Barrera** throughout the fight before winning via TKO in 11 rounds to snatch the latter's "The Ring" Featherweight (126 lbs) Mythical Crown. **Photo by Photobucket.com**

times. The second bout was another classic, with Pacquiao emerging as winner by TKO in the 10th round. The third fight was hardly a contest. Pacquiao overpowered Morales in 3 rounds.

Then a rematch with Barrera 4 years after their first ring date buried any remnant of a notion that Pacquiao might have caught Barrera in one of the latter's bad nights. This time, as the crowd chanted "Barre-run," Barrera showed little heart to dispute that notion. He lost to Pacquiao by unanimous decision.

In between these highly anticipated match-ups came Pacquiao's tussles against lesser known opponents, mostly Mexicans. Fans went on to confer on Manny Pacquiao a variety of name tags: Mexecutioner, Destroyer, Pambansang Kamao (national fist), etc. But the one that rings a bell to almost everyone was "The Pacman."

Almost deified at home, his fame grew across the globe. The Pacman was now a superstar. Even his non-title fights earned for him purses that made other boxers contending for titles green with envy. The HBO, which eventually worked with a parade of American promoters who now all wanted a piece of Pacquiao, embraced him like a long-lost brother. Men of commerce knew a prized talent when they saw one. In so short a time, Pacquiao had created commercial boom for promoters, media organizations, advertisers, businesses that needed endorsements, casino outlets, etc. At one time, promoter Bob Arum had called him a walking money machine.

Interviewed by Philippine media on his arrival from the US after the sensational win against Erik Morales in their rematch, Manny was honest, candid and tried—but failed—to be modest.

"If you were a reporter, how would you write the headline of your story?"

"Storm from the Pacific," he said, smiling.

This was 2006. In ten years of prize fighting, The Pacman had already gone quite a long way.

Erik Morales, left, fell down like a log after a furious exchange of blows with **Manny Pacquiao** during Round 2 of their third meeting in the ring on November 18, 2006 in Nevada, Las Vegas, USA. **Photo by Google Images**.

PART TWO: MORE THAN A BOXING ICON

We already know why Manny Pacquiao has what it takes to succeed. With courage, discipline, hard work and faith, one can also make the case that he would have emerged equally successful in any job apart from, or other than, boxing. The meaning of the lessons that can be learned from his life and career transcends boxing. His story is bigger than the sport. Let us briefly recapture that story.

Way To The Top—A Replay

Attracting attention and collecting fat paychecks even from non-title fights, Pacquiao got something, by way of an unsolicited advice, from WBC President Jose Sulaiman. Directed at the The Pacman, Sulaiman issued a statement saying, in part, that "boxers are immortalized by the belts they won, not by the money they earned."

Although Sulaiman did not appear to have moral suasion over Team Pacquiao, what happened next was that Pacquiao went into a belt-grabbing binge in such dramatic proportions not seen since Henry Armstrong did it in 1938.

BELT NO. 1: At the foot of **Manny Pacquiao's** ascent to the top of boxing is his winning world titles in 7 different weight divisions. On December 5, 1998 in Thailand, **Pacquiao**, 19, KO'd **Chatchai Sasakul** of Thailand in 7 rounds to win his first title—the WBC Flyweight (112 lbs) belt. **Photo clip from YouTube.com**

BELT NO. 2: **Manny Pacquiao** snatched his second world title in another division from IBF Super Bantamweight Champion **Lhenohonolo Ledwaba** of South Africa on June 23, 2001 in Las Vegas, USA. Pacquiao TKO'd Ledwaba in 6 rounds. **Photo by Photobucket.com**

After Pacquiao's knock out win over Mexican Jorge Solis (33-0-2 win-loss-draw record) on April 14, 2007, Freddie Roach, Pacquiao's coach and protector since 2001, bared what he saw in the future. "We will start collecting titles next year," he said.

First, Juan Manuel Marquez got the rematch he demanded from Pacquiao. They clashed for the second time on March 15, 2008. After 12 rounds of intense battle, the judges ruled, 2-1, in favor of Pacquiao. The result was as controversial as the first fight, and the issues they generated were just as contentious.

If the fight settled one thing, however, it was the transfer of the super featherweight belt from Marquez to Pacquiao.

Pacquiao thus elevated himself to an elite class of 3-division champions that included Sugar Shane Mosley, Julio Cesar Chavez, etc.

Three months later, on June 28, 2008, Pacquiao took away David Diaz's lightweight title via a ninth round stoppage. His waist brimmed with belts. He now had 4, and counting.

Six months later, on December 6, 2008, he jumped 2 divisions upwards to face Oscar De La Hoya at 147 pounds. He weighed just 130 pounds 9 months earlier. Many people thought the De La Hoya fight was crazy for the immense disparity in size between the two warriors. They expressed concern about Pacquiao being destroyed beyond repair by De La Hoya. But on fight night, their concern soon shifted to the bigger De La Hoya. Pacquiao battered Oscar before the latter gave up the fight and, eventually, his boxing career.

Pacquiao thus conquered 4 weight divisions in 10 months, all of them in blitzkrieg fashion.

He was not done, however. On May 5, 2009, he flattened Ricky Hatton in 2 rounds to wrest his 6th title in as many weight divisions. And, topping it all, after 6 months, he defeated welterweight champion Miguel Cotto on November 14, 2009, for a record 7 titles in 7 weight divisions.

No one in boxing history had accomplished what Pacquiao has done. Oscar De La Hoya, having won world titles in 6 different weight divi-

BELT NO. 3: On November 15, 2003 **Manny Pacquiao** pummeled **Marco Antonio Barrera** to submission and grabbed the latter's "The Ring" Featherweight (126 lbs) Mythical Crown. **Photo by Google Images.**

BELT NO. 4: On March 15, 2008, **Manny Pacquiao** defeated **Juan Manuel Marquez**, another Mexican legend, to win the WBC Super Featherweight (130 lbs) crown, his fourth, in Las Vegas, USA. **Photo by Google Images.**

BELT NO. 5: Referee **Vic Drakulich** waves his hands to make official the 9th round stoppage of the June 28, 2008 WBC Lightweight (135 lbs) title fight between **Manny Pacquiao** and **David Diaz** (on the floor). The win earned for Pacquiao his fifth division title. **Photo by Google Images.**

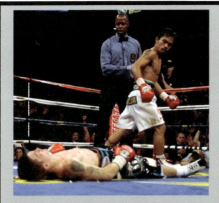

BELT NO. 6: On May 2, 2009, **Manny Pacquiao** dismantled UK's **Ricky Hatton** in 2 rounds in Las Vegas, USA, to win the IBO Light Welterweight (140 lbs) crown, his sixth . **Photo by Photobucket.com**

BELT NO. 7: On November 13, 2009, **Manny Pacquiao** knocked WBO Welterweight (147 lbs) champion **Miguel Cotto** of Puerto Rico twice enroute to winning the latter's title in Las Vegas, USA, to become the only boxer in history to win world titles in 7 different weight divisions. **Photo by Picsearch.com**

sions, comes closest to matching Pacquiao's achievement. But unlike De La Hoya who started at super feather-weight (130 lbs) and ended at middleweight (160 lbs), Pacquiao navigated a territory stretching over 41 lbs, from 106 to 147.

At the rate Pacquiao is trashing the competition; one wonders if there is anyone who can stop him. It seems—now or in the near future—no one is in sight.

POWER OF WILL

When American boxing fans first saw Pacquiao in 2001, he was fighting as a super bantamweight. He knocked out Ledwaba to snatch the latter's belt. At that time, Cotto had debuted as a pro at 139.5 pounds (light welterweight). Back then, it was unthinkable that a former super bantamweight would be facing a light welterweight. Indeed, at the time it was already braggadocio on his part to even challenge Barrera, who was then lord of all featherweights.

But Pacquiao went on to face not only a light welterweight. He went on to face a welterweight. He did not only face an ordinary welterweight. He faced an elite welterweight champion in Cotto.

Because of his amazing success in boxing, boxing

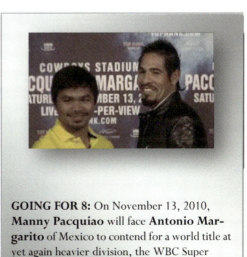

GOING FOR 8: On November 13, 2010, **Manny Pacquiao** will face **Antonio Margarito** of Mexico to contend for a world title at yet again heavier division, the WBC Super Welterweight (154 lbs) crown, possibly his eighth, in Dallas, Texas, USA. **Photo by**

fans are wont to ask: What makes The Pacman tick?

Some say he is a freak of nature. Others, such as the Mayweathers—believing that no living creature like him exists—have either implied or directly alleged that Pacquiao is taking illegal performance-enhancing drugs, or PEDs.

EARLIER, THIS BOOK has already cited the qualities that made Pacquiao the superb athlete that he is today. Let's go over them one more time.

First, he dreams and works on his dreams. Aside from his athletic gifts, much has been said about his legendary work ethic. He works harder in training camp than most of his competitors. This builds his stamina and further hones his skills.

The skills he has managed to develop overtime have been acknowledged by not a few boxing experts, such as Al Bernstein and Bert Sugar. Aside from his phenomenal hand and foot speed, Pacquiao has demonstrated success in launching attacks through uncanny angles and from all directions. Many observers concede that this offensive prowess has set Pacquiao apart from the rest of the greatest boxers.

That's not all. He seems to have eternity at his disposal when judging whether to unload, reload, or load on his punches. We are talking here of milliseconds, like seeing Kobe Bryant at the apex of his leap. To unload means to reconfigure the footwork, keep the balance, or maintain a position for defense or offense. To reload means to stick with jabs and hooks that either stop a hostile attack or to set up one's own assault. To load means to produce the right mix of mass and energy for arm and hip muscles behind a shot. The aim is to stun and take out the prey. If his preparation for a fight is adequate, he is that sharp. He does not only hit the opponent. He hits them at places where it hurts.

In his book "Jeet Kune Do," martial arts legend Bruce Lee said that the power of a punch comes from the hips. A lightweight fighter who harnesses this power can knockout more opponents than a heavyweight who doesn't.

Second, he has no fear inside the ring. Fighters do not acquire them through training. Either they have it or they don't. Courage makes it possible for Pacquiao to impose his will on his opponent. It allows him to commit to his punches and bring all his power behind them. It allows him to shift strategies (like fighting at close range the way he did against Cotto) which inferior fighters may find too risky to take.

In this fight against **Oscar De La Hoya** in 2008, **Manny Pacquiao** shows how to use full body weight to generate power behind his shot. Manny jumped over 2 weight divisions to face the 6-division titlist Oscar. Oscar took a beating and had to give up the fight at the end of 8th round, and eventually his golden boxing career. **Photo by Google Images.**

In his post-fight analysis, Philippine Star sports writer Quinito Henson said: "Pacquiao took a big gamble by leaning against the ropes to invite Cotto to whale away. Only a gutsy and fearless fighter would do it. Pacquiao once more showed how big his heart is and when you come down to it, that was the margin of difference."

Third, Pacquiao has tremendous will power. It is the root of his many other traits. He can compartmentalize his brain to focus on the task at hand. He finds order where others see chaos. While training for a fight, for example, he could work in the middle of a civil war. During fight night itself, he can be seen smiling as he enters the ring. But when the bell rings and the fighters are unleashed, his face turns serious, his jaws menacingly clinched.

Fourth, faith in His God has yet to be shaken. He genuinely believes in the power and benevolence of His God. Anything that happens from what he does, he leaves it all to God. He works and prays as hard as he could and believes that God will take care of the rest. He says: "Don't tell God you have a great problem. Tell your problem you have a great God."

Raised by a mother who once wished his son would become a priest, Pacquiao's piety had probably emerged out of filial obligation. Today, the priest-to-be-turned-boxer looks every inch a disciple of God.

The manifestation of his belief in God is elaborate. He is respectful and always tries to be humble, like he sees God in people. He glances upward to acknowledge and thank his benefactor, like saying God is up there, higher than human beings. He makes the sign of the cross every time he looks unsure of what's coming up, like saying "God, I'm yours. Let me be an instrument of your will."

In behavioral expressions that may never be understood by people who do not belong to his religious faith, or those who have little regard for his cultural moorings, his preferences could be construed as lacking in any scientifical-

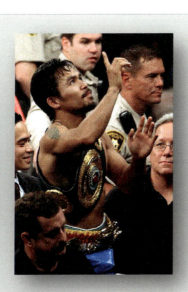 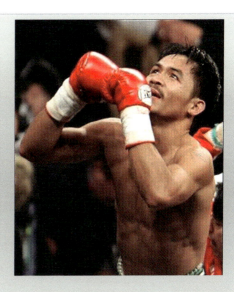

Manny Pacquiao says "If you believe in God, nothing is impossible". He tries to cheerfully acknowledge His God and show gratitude to Him every time there is opportunity for it. The reader may look at him and see if that faith is genuine or not. **Photos by Google Images.**

ly-coherent justification. Examples: Mandalay Bay over any other Las Vegas hotel; riding by car instead of by plane in going to Las Vegas from anywhere in the US; no to black clothing; female singers over male singers (except in the Ricky Hatton and Joshua Clottey fights) for the Philippine national anthem in his title fights, etc. And yes, after losing to Erik Morales in their first fight and blaming the blood test he took merely two days before the fight for what he deemed as sub-par performance, he has rejected subsequent demands for him to take any round of blood test so close to a fight. Where Samson in the Bible drew strength from his hair, Pacquiao feels something sacrosanct in this blood.

He also has a cute gesture that signifies his can-do spirit. No, it's not the sign of the cross or a back kick of the rope. Neither it is about him kneeling down in the solace of his corner, apparently deep in prayer. This is what he does: As the referee gathers both fighters in the middle of the ring for the final pre-fight instructions and the ceremonial glove shake, Pacquiao makes it a point to put his gloves on top of the opponents' gloves. That is how the power of symbolism and imagery works in the superstitious world of Manny Pacquiao.

STEROIDS?

Minutes after Pacquiao dethroned Miguel Cotto in Las Vegas, the crowd chanted "We want Floyd!" "We want Floyd!"

The fans voiced their choice. They made a noise about how Floyd Mayweather, Jr—whose retirement in 2007 gave way for Pacquiao to eventually supplant him at the mythical pound-for-pound throne—could possibly put up a real fight against the newly-crowned welterweight champion. In the days that followed, media generally referred to a possible Pacquiao-Mayweather match-up as the fight the world wanted to see.

Just a few weeks after the Pacquiao-Cotto fight, the potentially colossal Pacquiao-Mayweather clash (in terms of the amount of money and public interest experts believed it could generate) looked headed to reality. The relative ease by which the looming fistic duel progressed surprised those who expected lots of negotiating road blocks along the way, given the history of both fighters—and justified by how expensive their negotiators were—to demand every concession they could get from their opponents.

By the second week of December 2009, the HBO had already pegged a date for the bout: March 13, 2010. The venue (after Top Rank strongly pitched for Dallas Cowboys Stadium): MGM Grand, Las Vegas, USA.

Then came the killer blow. In a flash, a dispute over blood testing protocol erupted. The Mayweather camp demanded that an Olympic-style random

Floyd Mayweather Sr. (left), **Oscar De La Hoya** (middle) **and Richard Scheafer** (Right), among others, have either implied or alleged that **Manny Pacquiao** is a user of banned performance enhancing drugs. Pacquiao reacted by charging them in court for defamation. **Photos by Google Images.**

blood testing be conducted on both fighters. This meant that blood samples could be taken anytime, even on the day before or after the fight itself. The Pacquiao camp rejected the demand, saying that while random urinalysis and blood testing immediately after the fight were acceptable, it could not allow that blood samples be drawn at least 30 days before the fight. In his loss to Erik Morales in 2005, blood samples were drawn two days before the fight, and the Pacquiao camp used this argument to reject any blood testing so close to the day of the fight. Pacquiao himself explained that he felt weak during that Morales fight.

The Mayweather camp insisted that current drug testing methods being applied by the Athletic Commissions were inadequate. It stood firm on its demand for random blood testing, saying some performance enhancing drugs (PEDs), also loosely called steroids, cannot be detected from urine samples.

The US government agencies (like the State Athletic Commissions) that regulate professional boxing, among other contact sports, do not require blood samples for drug tests. Instead, they merely conduct urinalysis before and immediately after each fight.

The Mayweathers' position found a major endorser in the US Anti-Doping Agency (USADA), World Anti-Doping Agency's local arm in the US, whose Chief Executive, Travis Tygart, confirmed that there are *"performance enhancing drugs that only blood will detect.*

---

*To me, **Manny** is a real phenomenon. It's that he is so small and how he performs against bigger men, all of them tough. I'm talking about **Morales**, about **Barrera** and **Marquez**, even though **Marquez** gives **Manny** some problems in their matchup of styles.*

*I look at **Manny** as a lightweight and he's dominating the welterweights and now fighting at junior middleweight. His real weight, his true weight I think is 138 pounds. The rest of his pounds they just fill him up.*

*And another thing is that **Manny** does not dodge anybody. It's kind of crazy, all that a blown up lightweight has been accomplishing. He's been responsible for great fights against other great fighters.*

Like I said, there's no ducking of anyone. And no handpicked opponents who they know he can win easy against.

*(**Roberto**) **Duran** went up in weight, sure, but he was different than **Manny**. **Duran** was strictly a power puncher and guys who could box and move gave him big problems. This guy shows himself to be phenomenal because he can come in at you, take your punch and then clip you with that straight left hand.*

***Manny** can catch you coming in. He's got real hand speed but he also dares you to trade punches with him. He's got his own rhythm and he he's got that unique quick step. Duran would just walk in, wade into you. Manny can do that but he moves so quickly it's hard for the opponent to nail him*

--**Emmanuel Steward**, Boxing Trainer

Those include human growth hormone [HGH]; HBOC—and that is synthetic hemoglobin; transfusions; certain forms of EPO, such as Mircera, which is essentially a designer EPO... ."

Tygart has also been reported to have explained that scheduled or pre-arranged blood testing gives athletes who want to hide something time to mask the banned substances in their system. Thus unannounced testing, or random, is what makes the process effective.

Urinalysis can detect at least 40 substances that are prohibited pursuant to the World Anti-Doping Code (under the auspices of World Anti-Doping Agency, or WADA. The substances include anabolic agents (eg, Anabolic Androgenic Steroids); Peptide Hormones, Growth Factors and Related Hormones (eg, Erythropoiesis-Stimulating Agents [e.g. erythropoietin (EPO), darbepoetin (dEPO), methoxy polyethylene glycol-epoetin beta (CERA), hematide]; Chorionic Gonadotrophin and Luteinizing Hormone in males; Insulins; Corticotrophins; Growth Hormone [hGH], Insulin-like Growth Factor-1, Mechano Growth Factors, Platelet-Derived Growth Factor, Fibroblast Growth Factors, Vascular-Endothelial Growth Factor and Hepatocyte Growth Factor (HGF) as well as any other growth factor affecting muscle, tendon or ligament protein synthesis/degradation, vascularisation, energy utilization, regenerative capacity or fibre type switching; Platelet-derived preparations (e.g. Platelet Rich Plasma, "blood spinning") administered by intramuscular route); Beta-2 Agonists; Hormone Antagonists and Modulators; Diuretics and other masking agents. There are also prohibited methods. They include enhancement of oxygen transfer, chemical and physical manipulation, and gene doping.

In an article published by the "How Stuff Works"

The Proxy Pacquiao-Mayweather War

Although **Manny Pacquiao** and **Floyd Mayweather** Jr has yet to met in the ring, the last two fights involving both boxers happened (or will happen, in the case of Pacquiao vs Margarito (extreme right, above) largely as proxy to the highly anticipated Pacquiao-Mayweather bout. On November 12, 2009, a day before Manny Pacquiao dethroned Miguel Cotto as WBO Welterweight Champion, Floyd Mayweather held a press conference to announce his fight against Juan Manuel Marquez (second from left, above). "He could have waited for one day," said Freddie Roach, "and decide to fight the winner of the Pacquiao-Cotto if he wanted to." Floyd's decision to face Marquez drove Manny to face Joshua Clottey (extreme left, above). Meantime, Shane Mosley, whose January 2010 fight against Andre Berto was aborted, loomed all set as a substitute. After showing much reluctance in signing the fight contract against Mosley, Mayweather eventually fought Mosley (third from left, above) on May 1, 2010. Having won their respective bouts, fans once more egged the two on—like Micheal Buffer says—to rumble. They did not, due largely to what many people believed as Floyd's fear of Manny. Pacquiao went on to pick possibly the most challenging fight of his prize fighting career ever, against the much taller and stronger Margarito. **Photos by Google Images.**

website, Craig Freudenrich explains that "*hGH is a naturally occurring protein hormone produced by the pituitary gland and is important for normal human growth and development, especially in children and teenagers. Low hGH levels in children and teenagers result in dwarfism. Excessive hGH levels increase muscle mass by stimulating protein synthesis, strengthen bones by stimulating bone growth and reduce body fat by stimulating the breakdown of fat cells... Erythropoietin (EPO) is a naturally occurring protein hormone that is secreted by the kidneys during low-oxygen conditions. EPO stimulates the bone marrow stem cells to make red blood cells, which increase the delivery of oxygen to the kidney. Endurance athletes, such as those who compete in marathons, cycling or cross-country skiing, can use EPO to increase their oxygen supply by as much as seven to 10 percent.*"

Ryan Dunn, in an article also published online (Boxingnews24.com) reported that "*as far as the EPO known as Mircera goes, the reason it doesn't show up in the urine is because it breaks down in the body to molecules too large to pass through the kidneys. This makes it extremely difficult to detect in the urine, but it also means it stays in your body much longer. In fact, even a small dose of Mircera will stay in the body for an average of forty-two days. That means that, even with announced blood testing—as was requested by Manny Pacquiao in his recent negotiations with Floyd Mayweather Jr.—it would be impossible to cycle down during training and beat the tests.*"

Dunn also reported that a new testing method—NanoTrap—using urinalysis, has been proven to be more effective than blood testing insofar as detecting hGH was concerned. In sum, he advanced the proposition that given the availability of new testing methods, Pacquiao's position of blood testing not earlier than 30 days before the fight (EPO remains in body for more than that period of time) with random urinalysis (NanoTrap detects hGH) addressed Mayweather's concerns for ensuring a fair fight against somebody he had accused to be a cheater.

Dr. Don Catlin, founder of the UCLA Olympic Analytical Lab and the LA-based Anti-Research and in-charge of blood testing for hGH at the Beijing Olympics, weighed in on the controversy by saying that he seriously questioned the effectiveness of blood testing used by WADA and USADA. Although available since the 2004 Athens Olympics, the "capture rate" of said test had been found dismal.

Sports fans in general who are interested in promoting integrity in athletic competition, as well as in raising awareness on health risks that come with PEDs, may find the September 2000 report by The US CASA National Commission on Sports and Substance Abuse titled "Winning at Any Cost: Doping in Olympic Sports" illuminating. It recommended, among other things, that more research be conducted determine the

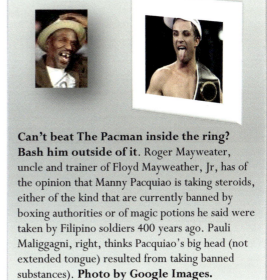

Can't beat The Pacman inside the ring? Bash him outside of it. Roger Mayweater, uncle and trainer of Floyd Mayweather, Jr, has of the opinion that Manny Pacquiao is taking steroids, either of the kind that are currently banned by boxing authorities or of magic potions he said were taken by Filipino soldiers 400 years ago. Pauli Maliggagni, right, thinks Pacquiao's big head (not extended tongue) resulted from taking banned substances). **Photo by Google Images.**

long-term consequences of use of performance-enhancing substances.

EXASPERATED OVER THE IMPASSE between the negotiating parties, Top Rank's Bob Arum advised Mayweather to raise the matter of imposing more stringent drug testing procedures with the State Commissions. The appropriate bodies, after all, had under their command adequate information and methods by which issues of that kind could be resolved.

Commenting on the botched negotiations, Arum said he could allow "*the same people that test the National Football League players and the National Basketball Association players among others to do the tests because they are used to dealing with professional athletes and they (Mayweather's camp) refused.*" He went further: "*The same USADA which tested nearly 200 American athletes (boxers, swimmers and track and field athletes) before they went to the Olympic Games "took nil, zero, zero blood tests and they want to take seven from our little Filipino. Now what the hell is going on? ... Let the Nevada State Athletic Commission recommend. Nobody appointed Mayweather as super Commissioner.*"

By the first week of January 2010, the dispute went through a mediation process that hardly changed the positions of either camp. The Mayweather camp yielded an inch by allowing a 14-day clearance (meaning blood will not be drawn 14 days before the fight). The Pacquiao camp, on the other hand, also yielded an inch by agreeing to a 24-day clearance. In the end, both camps still failed to meet halfway.

Pacquiao's representatives in the fight negotiations, mainly Arum, eventually shelved the Mayweather fight and went on to produce Joshua Clottey as Pacquiao's opponent for the March 13, 2010 fight date. For his part, Mayweather—by way of a fortuitous event that involved Shane Mosley (whose January 30 fight against Haitian Andre Berto had crumbled following the January 17, 2010 killer quake in Haiti—found himself zugzwanged in an unavoidable collision course versus Mosley. And so it came to pass: Pacquiao fought Clottey on March 13 at Dallas Cowboys, Texas, and Mayweather faced Mosley on May 1, 2010 at Las Vegas, both in the USA. Both Pacquiao and Mayweather Jr went on to defeat their respective opponents.

And yet, despite the on-going hoopla surrounding the two pairs of match-ups involving Pacquiao and Mayweather Jr, media continued to harp on the blood testing dispute that tripped the Pacquiao-Mayweather fight and its contentious backdrop: the charges of steriods use aimed by the Mayweathers at Pacquiao.

The weeks that followed Pacquiao's dismantling of Ricky Hatton in two rounds in May 2009 saw Floyd Mayweather Sr (who lost no time in blaming Hatton for the debacle, saying Hatton failed to follow his instructions) making public his allegations that Pacquiao was on steroids. Hatton earlier hired Mayweather Sr as Chief Trainer and Cornerman for the Pacquiao fight.

Mayweather Sr launched his attacks through media interviews. And as he pressed his offensive, it became clear he also meant to put in doubt the authenticity of Pacquiao's achievements inside the ring. The rest of the Mayweathers—notably Roger, Jeff and Floyd Jr, along with several other boxing personalities—also made public their opinion that, in jest, Pacquiao could not be the great fighter that he has become without the aid of PEDs.

For his part, Pacquiao dismissed the accusations as untrue. "I don't even know what they (drugs) look like," he said. Having been subjected to tests for banned substances in more than 9 years (from 2001 to 2009) that he has fought in the US, he had reason to be proud of his unblemished laboratory record. He felt thoroughly offended by the Mayweather-led assault on his name. Claiming that he had a right to protect his integrity and affirm the value of the work he put into the sport, he decided—after weeks of tormented introspection (the charge sheet would say)—to eventually sue the Mayweathers, along with Golden Boy Promotions, for defamation.

Within days following the filing of the lawsuit in Las Vegas, USA, the Mayweathers modified their public attack: From Pacquiao on steroids to Pacquiao with magical potions.

Interviewed on Boxing Truth Radio, USA, Roger Mayweather said: "*That mother***** is on the A-side meth, that's what the f*** he's on… It's called the A-side meth. He on that or he on something else. The A-side meth is what they used to have 500 years ago. Remember when the Philippines were fighting the US soldiers? They were shooting them motherf****s with 45s. And 45s were bouncing off their motherf****ng a$$. They weren't even dying!*"

But while such a contention may have lacked factual basis (for example: the American soldiers invaded the Philippines in 1898, and not 500 years ago), it did not lack supporters.

Floyd Sr joined brother Roger in bashing Pacquiao: "*He can't beat Clottey without that sh*t in him. Even though he was dehydrated, he couldn't beat De La Hoya without that sh*t. He couldn't beat Ricky Hatton without that sh*t and he couldn't beat Cotto without that sh*t. I don't even think he could beat that kid from Chicago [David Diaz] without that sh*t. He wouldn't be able to beat any of the guys without enhancement drugs, that's what I think. My belief is my opinion and you cannot change it. I know one thing, little Floyd will fight him fair.*" He explained further: "*It's not a steroid. It's something from the Philippines. Something they use in the army. When you hit the guy with a .45 or a .38 and they keep coming after they get shot.*

Whatever it is it has to be something strong for you to keep coming forward after you get shot."

Floyd Jr himself had not run out of theses to indict Pacquiao. Several times he had been quoted by media as saying that Pacquiao "*was an ordinary fighter who became a pound for pound sensation as he got older.*" He went on to elaborate: "*In a fighter's career, a fighter starts off good and he's good until the end of his career or a fighter starts off good and then goes downhill towards the end of his career. A fighter doesn't start off like Manny Pacquiao, just ordinary, and then once he gets over the age of 25 he becomes an extra-ordinary fighter. It just doesn't work like that in this sport of boxing… So I just want to know what is it really? That's all I want to know, what is it really?*"

Indeed, none of the Mayweathers could seem to figure out what it was. At first they thought it was because of illegal drugs. Then they thought Pacquiao was loaded with talisman.

What some people might have forgotten—and Floyd Jr included (obviously), is that there had been extraordinary fighters who started looking like ordinary boxers. Henry Armstrong, coming strong at number three in the all-time greats list which will be shown later in this book, was one of them.

Early in his career, Armstrong hardly made an impression he would go on to become one of the world's greatest fighters. He had an average start: 4 losses and 5 draws in his first 23 fights. His next 21 bouts were equally unimpressive, again losing 4 times and drawing once. By this time, he had compiled a 30-8-6 win-loss-draw record in 44 professional fights.

Another example is Benny Leonard, who is also a consistent all-time greats lister. Leonard launched his professional boxing career at 15 in 1911, got knocked out in his first fight, but came back to become one of the greatest lightweights in boxing history. When the press minted the term "pound for pound champion" in the early 20th century, it was meant to refer to him.

But like Armstrong who would follow in his footsteps 3 decades later, Leonard struggled in the early years of his professional career. After 54 fights, he barely managed to win 28 of them, losing 11, and the rest were either draws or no contests.

We may also add Bernard Hopkins as another example. BHops started to make a mark as a fighter only in his late 30s.

There are other examples. But have been cited should suffice to raise doubts on the accuracy of Mayweather Jr's claim that ordinary fighters could not rise to become extra-ordinary.

Many people will also find it inaccurate to say Pacquiao started out as an ordinary fighter.

Despite losing twice (both inside the distance) early in his boxing career, Manny Pacquiao had compiled a boxing record that only Floyd Jr can describe as ordinary.

At 19, he was already a world flyweight champion. By direct comparison, Mayweather had yet to beat a world-class fighter at this age. As a footnote, though, Mayweather did win the Bronze Medal (Featherweight Class) at the Atlanta Olympics. (Both Pacquiao and Mayweather weighed 106 pounds at age 16, but Mayweather

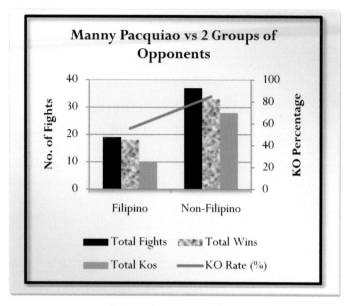

balooned to 131 pounds at age 19 (compared to Manny who weighed 112 lbs at this age). The huge disparity in rates at which they grew as teenagers **could be** explained by their racially-defined genetic make up, and should not be by something else, in case one gets too wild with the innuendo that the Mayweathers might have been drugs users themselves.

Aside from the unprecedented levels of achievement that Pacquiao has scaled inside the ring, one may note that—for non-Filipino boxers in particular—he has a frightening knock out rate. Pacquiao's career knockout rate (wins inside the distance over total wins) is 76 percent. But against non-Filipino opponents, his knockout rate zooms up to 90 percent.

Thus only a Mayweather could reconcile the foregoing facts with the notion that, one, ordinary fighters cannot rise to become extra-ordinary and, two, Pacquiao was—early in his career—ordinary. At the very least, the data could suggest many things. And one of them tended to show that Pacquiao could knock out an opponent anytime he wanted to.

PACQUIAO VS MAYWEATHER 2

No, there wasn't any bout between Manny Pacquiao and Floyd Mayweather Jr inside the ring, much less a second one.

But due to pressure from boxing fans, and the promise of big bucks it offers those who work on the business side of the sport, at least two rounds of negotiations (depending on whose side of story telling the reader may want to believe) between the camps of Pacquiao and Mayweather took place. But both negotiations, as the public now knows, have failed to deliver any Pacquiao-Mayweather ring match-up. Pacquiao and Mayweather occupy the top two spots in almost all pound for pound lists today, and the public's fascination for their live ring match up is in large measure driven by the need to answer the question of who is truly superior between the two of them.

The first round of negotiations took place in December 2009—following Pacquiao's demolition of Cotto a month earlier (Mayweather had beaten Juan Manuel Marquez two months earlier). It went pfft, as has been discussed above, due to irreconcilable disagreements on the drug testing protocol. If there was one thing both camps did agree on, however, it was in seeking a third-party mediation.

The mediation succeeded in reducing Pacquiao's demand for a drug-testing window (the period after which no further drug testing would be conducted heading to the day of the fight) from 30 days to 24 days. For Mayweather, this was not enough. He demanded that random tests be conducted as close as 14 days before the day of the fight.

The second round of negotiations supposedly took place between May and July of 2010—following Mayweather's unanimous decision win over Shane Mosley on May 1 (Pacquiao had clipped Joshua Clottey two months earlier). This time Pacquiao was reported to have agreed to the 14-day window demanded by the Mayweather.

On the other hand, based on reports that may have been understood as saying different things, Mayweather ignored Pacquiao's concession and in effect dashed, once more, the immediate possibility of any Pacquiao-Mayweather fight.

The Mayweather camp (represented by Floyd's advisers and Golden Boy Promotions) later issued a statement saying to the effect that no second round of negotiations took place. The Pacquiao camp (represented by Top Rank Promotions), on the other hand, asserted the opposite: that negotiations did take place. It further went on record, mainly through Top Rank, that Mayweather's fear of the Pacman and the legal problems its training team faced at the time, may have prevented Mayweather from signing the fight contract.

Probably concerned that the boxing public might have gotten tired of the disappearing Pacquiao-Mayweather saga, Ross Greenberg, the HBO president for sports, came out with a statement saying that negotiations between the two camps did take place.

"I had been negotiating with a representative from each side since May 2nd, carefully trying to put the fight together. Hopefully, someday this fight will happen. Sports fans deserve it," Greenberg said.

As things stand now, it seems Manny Pacquiao is winning not only his ring battles. He is also poised, where the Mayweather tussle is concerned, to grab the credibility challenge title as well.

He has become more than a boxing hero.

Part Three: The Greatest Of All Time

This book understands the risks of hu-hum in saying that Manny Pacquiao is the greatest fighter of all time. The GOAT (Greatest Of All Time) debate is far from settled and thousands, possibly millions, more among boxing fans would have their own opinions. But let no one lose sight of the rules: In this debate, there is no right or wrong contention; there are only strong or weak arguments.

From here on in, this book shall try to present the reasons why it says Manny Pacquiao is the greatest pound for pound boxer of all time.

Boxing Through The Years

There are historical accounts that suggest the existence of boxing in Africa long before the Romans roared and thundered with chants and excitement while watching the deadly matches among gladiators at their famed coliseum. Solid documentation, however, indicates that boxing as a sport and form of entertainment has—like civilization itself—originated from Europe. The Greeks for centuries have been known to fight with their fist as a form of sporting contest. By the 18th century, England has already devised the word "boxing" to distinguish it as a form of sporting competition apart from fistfights where the primary concern was to settle disputes among combatants. The basic rules—such as use of a ring and fighting within an agreed number of rounds—that governed the sport emerged and gained wide acceptance.

In the olden days there was only one champion. It was hardly surprising then that the relatively bigger boxers constituted the sport's cream of the crop, as it were. Boxing matches "tailor-made" for lighter boxers did occur since mid 18th century, but they at best fitted under the category of exhibition bouts. Although deemed professional in the sense that fighters—both heavy and light—fought for money rather than for anything else, no specific championship awaited the winners at the lighter bouts. The word "light weight" in fact did not form part of the boxing vocabulary until the 19th century.

Eventually, use of the terms "lightweight," "welterweight," "middleweight" and "heavyweight" would become commonplace, but in the main each of them still needed a universally-recognized definition. By the 20th century, boxing rules would introduce new weight classes, like straw weight and even up to super heavyweight (at some point certain weight classes would disappear, only to re-emerge at another time). At any rate, consensus over their definitions has often remained a problem.

In mid-19th century, boxing evolved into what would soon become the professional

Bob Sitzsimmons, a middleweight, won the heavyweight title in 1897 and set a boxing record that remained intact for more than a century, until **Roy Jones, Jr,** also a middleweight, won the heavyweight crown in 2003. **Photo by Sports Illustrated.**

sport that it is today. The 1853 "Rules of the London Prize-Ring" introduced new sets of contest regulations. Boxing has, by this time, gained popularity as a "pugilistic" contest. Pugilism was also known as bare-knuckle fighting. Here, combatants wore no gloves. London's Pugilistic Benevolent Society further amended the rules in 1866 and, a year later, John Chambers formulated what came to be known as "Queensberry Rules." These rules provided for a more comprehensive set of regulations that governed the conduct of boxing.

The Queensberry Rules had 12 key provisions. They required, among other things, that matches should be conducted in "a fair stand-up boxing match" inside a 24-foot ring. Three minutes were to be allocated for each round; and boxers could rest for a full minute in between rounds. A boxer who went down from a legitimate punch had ten seconds within which to get up and resume fighting; otherwise he loses the match by knockout. Boxers were allowed to wear "fair-size" gloves (to protect the knuckles). They were not allowed to "wrestle or hug."

Boxing throughout history had largely been a male sport. But few matches involving women boxers occurred as early as the 18th century. Organized boxing for women came to life during the later part of the 20th century.

Towards the end of the 19th century, the days of pugilism (bare-knuckle "Prize Ring") gradually ended. Standard boxing that evolved from the Queensberry Rules took its place. In the meantime, amateur boxing increasingly gained popularity in schools, armed forces and even in urban centers in England.

AMATEUR BOXING

Moral questions hounded professional boxing from the day it was born. The sport attracted controversy—then and as it is now—and the indictment it appeared to come mostly from the relatively well-off members of society, since the rather tabloid commentary at the time went to the effect that some sectors resented the way the working class—from whose ranks most of boxing's practitioners came—was profiting from it. The insinuation was that some kind of "class war" brewed somewhere. Also, controversial fight outcomes—like some fighters being suspected of taking a "dive," or even defaulting some matches—that marred the conduct of professional boxing further helped the critics argue their case. At any rate, what could be said on a less sensational note was that those who saw the need to make boxing less cruel and less commercialized have, over the years, comprised a growing constituency. Thus by the late 1800s, amateur boxing was on its way having its consequential share of followers.

Various governing bodies for amateur boxing emerged as the sport progressed, such as the Amateur Boxing Association (1880) in England, the International Olympic Boxing Federation (established in Paris in 1920), and the International Amateur Boxing Association (London, 1946). Today, almost each country has its own governing body or bodies for amateur boxing. In the United States, there is the Amateur Athletic Union (AAU), the Golden Gloves Association, and USA Boxing.

Key amateur boxing rules fixed, among other things, the duration for each bout, for example male boxers could box 4 x 2-minute rounds or 3 x 3-minute rounds by agreement. Females could box 4 x 2-minute rounds by agreement. In Open Championships and international tournaments, males boxed 3 x 3-minute rounds while females boxed 4 x 2-minute rounds. The standard one-minute rest in between rounds was in effect.

Amateur boxing debuted as an Olympic event in 1904 Olympic Games and has since then been a part of the Olympic Games (except in the 1912 Games). Computerized scoring in the Olympics started in 1992, where at least three out of five judges were required to simultaneously press the scoring button so that a point could be credited to any boxer who, in their view, landed a clean blow.

Many professional boxers who rose in stature and fame were, in their younger days, outstanding amateur boxers themselves. The likes of Sugar Ray Robinson, Cassius Clay (Muhammad Ali) and Oscar De La Hoya belonged to this classification.

THE SANCTIONING BODIES OF PROFESSIONAL BOXING

But despite the decline of bare-knuckle prize-fighting and the rise in popularity of amateur boxing, the appeal of professional boxing especially among hardcore fight fans was for so long a time hardly diminished. On the contrary, professional boxing (applying the Queensberry Rules), has gradually spread from the United Kingdom to the rest of the world. Also, the need for more effective regulations and regulating bodies governing the sport grew in significance.

London's Pugilistic Benevolent Society retooled itself in 1918 and came to be known as the British Board of Boxing Control (BBoBC). It further went re-structuring in 1929 and slightly shuffled its name to become the British Boxing Board of Control. Since the 1920s, the BBBoC, alongside the National Boxing Association (USA), the New York State Athletic Commission and the International Boxing Union, comprised the world's dominant sanctioning bodies that regulated the sport as well as recognized and/or awarded world boxing titles, among other functions.

The 1867 Marquess of Queensberry Rules

1. To be a fair stand-up boxing match in a twenty-four foot ring or as near that size as practicable.
2. No wrestling or hugging allowed.
3. The rounds to be of 3 minutes duration and 1 minute time between rounds.
4. If either man fall through weakness or otherwise, he must get up unassisted, ten seconds be allowed to do so, the other man meanwhile to return to his corner; and when the fallen man is on his legs the round is to be resumed and continued until the three minutes have expired. If one man fails to come to the scratch in the ten seconds allowed, it shall be in the power of the referee to give his award in favour of the other man.
5. A man hanging on the ropes in a helpless state, with his toes off the ground, shall be considered down.
6. No seconds or any other person to be allowed in the ring during the rounds.
7. Should the contest be stopped by any unavoidable interference, the referee (is) to name the time and place as soon as possible for finishing the contest, to that the match can be won and lost, unless the backers of the men agree to draw the stakes.
8. The gloves to be fair-sized boxing gloves of the best quality and new.
9. Should a glove burst, or come off, it must be replaced to the referee's satisfaction.
10. A man on one knee is considered down, and if struck is entitled to the stakes.
11. No shoes or boots with springs allowed.
12. The contest in all other respects to be governed by the revised rules of the London Prize Ring.

Source: BoxRec Wikepedia

Professional boxing flourished wherever commerce boomed. The rise of the United States as an economic power created business opportunities for prizefighting, and for boxing entrepreneurs to cash in on them. One such boxing visionary and apparently a strategic manager, Tex Rickard, established in early 1900s the Madison Square Garden Corporation as a boxing promoter and built the Madison Square Garden in New York, USA, as venue for boxing matches. Some megafights involving Jack Dempsey, Gene Tunney, Joe Louis, (all of whom were, at one time or another, under the promotional outfit founded by Rickard) among others, took place at the Garden. At a time when pay-per-view and satellite TV were yet unheard of, the Garden could generate millions of dollars from a single night of boxing. Largely because of this, the Garden would in time earn the title of "Mecca of boxing."

But as controversies hounded the sport once more (for example, Jack Dempsey won the heavyweight title from Jess Willard but did not get paid because his manager lost his purse on a bet that Dempsey would knock Willard out in the first round) the burgeoning business of boxing neces-

Modern Rules of Boxing

1. The rules of boxing vary from jurisdiction to jurisdiction, and on whether it is an amateur or professional bout. A violation of the following rules is considered a foul, and can result in a point deduction or disqualification:

2. You cannot hit below the belt, hold, trip, kick, bite, headbutt, wrestle, spit on, or push your opponent; you cannot hit with your head, shoulder, forearm, or elbow; you cannot hit with an open glove, the inside of the glove, the wrist, the backhand, or the side of the hand.

3. You cannot punch your opponent's back, or the back of his head or neck (rabbit punch), or on the kidneys (kidney punch).

4. You cannot throw a punch while holding on to the ropes to gain leverage.

5. You can't hold your opponent and hit him at the same time, or duck so low that your head is below your opponent's belt line.

6. When the referee breaks you from a clinch, you have to take a full step back; you cannot immediately hit your opponent--that's called "hitting on the break" and is illegal.

7. You cannot spit out your mouthpiece on purpose to get a rest.

8. If you score a knockdown of your opponent, you must go to the farthest neutral corner while the referee makes the count.

9. If you "floor" your opponent, you cannot hit him when he's on the canvas. A floored boxer has up to ten seconds to get back up on his feet before losing the bout by knockout.

10. A boxer who is knocked down cannot be saved by the bell in any round, depending upon the local jurisdiction's rules.

11. A boxer who is hit with an accidental low blow has up to 5 minutes to recover. If s/he cannot continue after five minutes, s/he is considered knocked out.

12. If the foul results in an injury that causes the fight to end immediately, the boxer who committed the foul is disqualified.

13. If the foul causes injury but the bout continues, the referee orders the judges to deduct two points from the boxer who caused the injury.

14. If an unintentional foul causes the bout to be stopped immediately, the bout is ruled a "no contest" if four rounds have not been fully completed. (If the bout was scheduled for four rounds, then three rounds must have been completed.) If four rounds have been completed, the judges' scorecards are tallied and the fighter who is ahead on points is awarded a technical decision. If the scores are even, it will be called a "technical draw."

15. If a boxer is knocked out of the ring, he gets a count of 20 to get back in and on his feet. He cannot be assisted.

16. In some jurisdictions the standing eight-count or the three knockdown rule also may be in effect. In other jurisdictions, only the referee can stop the bout.

Source: BoxRec Wikipedia

sitated order. The Senate of New York enacted in 1920 the Walker Law (from its author Senator James Walker) that not only affirmed the legal standing of professional boxing in New York, but also provided for a new set of boxing rules, including rules on weight divisions. The Walker Law impacted on the rest of the boxing world, as more American States promulgated their own boxing rules and regulations, which often used the Walker Law as basis or guide.

The New York State Athletic Commission (NYSAC)

The State of New York in the USA established the NYSAC in 1920 pursuant to the provisions of the Walker Law, which regulated the conduct of boxing and wrestling in that State. The functions of the NYSAC included issuing of licenses, supervising of promoters, professional boxers and wrestlers, kick boxers, mixed martial arts fighters, ring officials, corner men, matchmakers, and the like.

In 1929 the NYSAC institutionalized 13 weight classes, namely: 1) Junior Flyweight (109 pounds); 2) Flyweight (112 pounds); 3) Junior Bantamweight (115 pounds); 4) Bantamweight (118 pounds); 5) Junior Featherweight (122 pounds); 6) Featherweight (126 pounds); 7) Junior Lightweight (130 pounds); 8) Lightweight (135 pounds); 9) Junior Welterweight (140 pounds); 10) Welterweight (147 pounds); 11) Middleweight (160 pounds); 12) Light Heavyweight (175 pounds); and, 13) Heavyweight (unlimited).

The NYSAC published (Self-Defense Sporting Annual 1929, p. 14), also in 1929, the new set of rules and regulations, an excerpt of which follows:

Referee

The referee shall have the power:

(a) To cast the third vote, in which case the three votes shall be of equal value. In the event of two votes coinciding, the result shall be so determined. In the event of all votes disagreeing, the contest shall be declared a draw.

(b) To stop a bout or contest at any stage and make a decision if he considers it too one-sided.

(c) To stop a bout or contest if he considers the competitors are not in earnest. In this case he may disqualify one or both contestants.

(d) To disqualify a contestant who commits a foul and to award decision to opponent.

The referee shall not touch the contesting boxers, except on failure of one or both contestants to obey the "break" command.

When a contestant is "down" the referee and timekeeper shall at once commence calling off the seconds and indicating the count with a motion of the arm. If the contestant fails to rise before count of ten, the referee shall declare him the loser.

Should a contest who is "down" arise before count of ten is reached and again go down intentionally, without being struck, the referee and timekeeper shall resume count where it left off.

Should a contestant leave the ring during the one minute rest period between rounds and fail to be in ring when gong rings to resume boxing, the referee shall count him out, the same as if he were "down."

If a contestant is down, his opponent shall retire to the farthest corner and remain there until the count is completed.

Should he fail to do so, the referee and timekeeper may cease counting until he has so retired.

Referee shall decide all questions arising during a contest which are not specifically covered by these rules.

Judges

The two judges shall be stationed at opposite sides of the ring. The decisions of the judges shall be based primarily on effectiveness, taking into account the following points:

Notes On Evolution Of The 17 Weight Classes

From 2 divisions in the 18th century, there are now 17 weight divisions. Each of the division has its own story, as presented below:

- Heavyweight—first originated as 160 pounds plus by Jack Broughton (in 1738); established by the ABA as unlimited (in 1889); reaffirmed as no limit by the NSC (in 1909); changed by the NYSAC to 175 plus in 1920; modified again in 1979 by the WBC (followed by the WBA in 1982 and the IBF in 1983); again modified in 2004 by the WBA, WBC and IBF to mean 201-plus pounds.
- Cruiserweight (also called junior heavyweight)—first originated in England (later called lighter-heavyweight); established as 176-190 lbs by the WBC in 1979, then the WBA in 1982, and the IBF in 1983; modified in 2004 first by the WBC, then the WBA and next by the IBF to allow a maximum limit of 200 pounds.
- NOTE: the English class Cruiserweights (from 1889-1937) became Light Heavyweight (1937-present). The name reappeared in America (in 1980) for a new class of 190, then 195 and now 200 lbs.
- Light Heavyweight (also called lighter-heavyweight)—initially created by Lou Houseman for his fighter Jack Root (in 1903); first established by the NSC (in 1909) as 12 stone, 7 pounds or 175 lbs.
- Super Middleweight (also called Junior Light Heavyweight)—first established in Salt Lake City, Utah in 1967; re-established by the Ohio Boxing Commission (in 1974); "resurrected" by the World Athletic Association (in 1982); recognized by the IBF (in 1984); then the WBA (in 1987): and last by the WBC (in 1988).
- Middleweight—first established by the ABA as 11 stone, 4 pounds (in 1889); modified by the NSC (in 1909) as 11 stone, 6 pounds or 160 lbs.
- Junior Middleweight (also called Light Middleweight, Super Welterweight)—first created by the Walker Law (in 1920); established by the NBA (in 1956); universally accepted by the Austrian Boxing Council and European Boxing Union (in 1962).
- NOTE: this weight class can be divided into two historical periods: 1956-1962 and 1963-present.
- Welterweight—first recognized in England as 142-145 pounds (in 1889, then 1892); Established by the NSC (in 1909) as 10 stone, 7 pounds or 147 lbs and made uniform as 147 pounds by the NYSAC and NBA (in 1920).
- Junior Welterweight—first created by the Walker Law; recognized by Boxing Blade and also sanctioned by the NBA (in 1922); established by the WBC in 1968. NOTE: This weight class can be divided into three distinct historical periods: 1922-1930, 1946-1959, and 1968-present.
- Lightweight—first originated as any fighter whose weight was less than 160 pounds by Jack Broughton (in 1738); under London Prize Ring, weight class ranged from (130-150); established by the ABA as 10 stone (in 1889); modified by the NSC (in 1909) as 9 stone, 9 pounds or 135 lbs.
- Junior Lightweight—created by the Walker Law, established by the NYSAC (in 1930). NOTE: this weight class can be divided into distinct historical periods: 1921-1933 and 1959-present.
- Featherweight—first created under London Prize Ring Rules (in 1860) as 118 lbs (53.6 kg or 8 stone, 6 pounds); established by the ABA as 126 lbs (57.3 kg or 9 stone in 1889); changed under Marquess Rules to 110 lbs (in 1889); changed to 115 pounds (52.3 kg or 8 stone, 3 pounds) when George Dixon beat Cal McCarthy in 1890; his manager then changed to 120 lbs (54.4 kg or 8 stone, 8 pounds) when Dixon beat Abe Willis; modified by the NSC (in 1909) as 126 lbs (57.3 kg or 9 stone).
- Junior Featherweight—first created by the Walker Law, though not fully established by the NYSAC; sanctioned by WBC (in 1976).
- Bantamweight—first established by the ABA; fully sanctioned by the NSC (in 1909) as 118 lbs (53.6 kg or 8 stone, 6 pounds); later solidified by the Walker Law for standardized weight divisions (in 1920); endorsed by the NYSAC, and sanctioned by the NBA. Under London Prize Ring Rules, the weight division was 105 lbs (47.7 kg or 7 stone, 7 pounds). Increased to 112 lbs (50.9 kg or 8 stone in 1880) and then 115 pounds (52.3 kg or 8 stone, 3 pounds in 1890) under Queensberry Rules. The weight class was set at 116 pounds (52.7 kg or 8 stone, 4 pounds in 1898). The present 118 pound limit was first adopted in England (in 1904), then by the NSC (in 1909).
- Junior Bantamweight—first created by the Walker Law (in 1920).
- Flyweight—first established by the NSC (in 1909) as 112 lbs (50.9 kg or 8 stone). English boxing authorities followed suit and set the weight limit as 108 lbs (49.1 kg or 7 stone, 10 lbs in 1910). United States boxing commissions NBA and NYSAC recognized this weight class (in 1927). New York's Walker Law established the weight class (in 1920) as 112 pounds.
- Junior Flyweight—first established by the Walker Law; sanctioned by the WBC in 1975.
- Strawweight (also called Minimumweight, Mini-Flyweight)—first established by the IBF (in 1987) and later recognized by both the WBA and WBC (in 1988).
- Paperweight—first established by the Queensberry Amateur Championship and ABA as 95 lbs and less (in 1880). In time the paperweight champion became synonymous with the flyweight and bantamweight champions, although the weight actually increased 17 pounds by sanctioning of the NSC around 1896-1898.

Source: BoxRec Wikipedia

1. A clean, forceful hit, landed on any vulnerable part of the body above the belt should be credited in proportion to its damaging effect.

2. Aggressiveness is next in importance and points should be awarded to the contestant who sustains the action of a round by the greatest number of skillful attacks.

3. Defensive work is relatively important and points should be given for cleverly avoiding or blocking a blow.

4. Points should be awarded where ring generalship is conspicuous. They comprise such points as the ability to quickly grasp and take advantage of every opportunity offered, the capacity to cope with all kinds of situations which may arise; to foresee and neutralize an opponent's method of attack; to force an opponent to adopt a style of boxing at which he is not particularly skillful.

5. It is advisable to deduct points when a contestant persistently delays the action of a contest by clinching and lack of aggressiveness.

6. Points should be deducted for a foul even though it is unintentional and not of a serious nature to warrant disqualification.

7. A contestant should be given credit for sportsmanlike actions in the ring, close adherence to the spirit as well as the letter of the rules and for refraining from taking technical advantage of situations unfair to an opponent.

8. In order to arrive at a true conclusion every point should be carefully observed and noted as the contest progresses, the decision going to the)contestant who scores the greatest number of effective points regardless of the number of rounds won or lost.

When neither contestant has a decided margin in effectiveness, the winner should be determined on points scored and aggressiveness.

In 1922, the NYSAC ruled that boxers aged below 20 could not be part of a boxing match requiring more than 6 rounds.

National Boxing Association

As New York solidified its status as hub of professional boxing, the other American states decided not to be left behind. In 1921, or one year after the NYSAC came into being, 17 (other accounts say 13) American states, converged to erect the National Boxing Association (NBA) in Rhode Island. The concerted act was, in many ways, designed to neutralize the growing influence of the NYSAC over professional boxing not only in the US but throughout the world. Twenty years later, all boxing matches in America were sanctioned by the NBA, except in New York and Massachusetts.

One of the more memorable fights sanctioned by the NBA involved Jack Dempsey in his matches against Firpo, Carpetier and his tormentor, Gene Tunney.

There were instances, particularly within the 1927-1940 period, where both the NYSAC and the NBA recognized different world champions coming from the same weight division, creating confusion among fight fans at the time. By 1962, the NBA had metamorphosed to become the present-day World Boxing Association. A year later, in 1963, the NYSAC helped deliver the birth of the World Boxing Council. And so the rivalry between the NYSAC and the NBA continued.

World Boxing Association

Half-way through the 20th century, with two devastating World Wars and a global economic recession still fresh in the peoples' minds, the world needed a break. Reconstruction and economic recovery was high in the global agenda. In time, though, peoples around the world picked themselves up and gradually regained their affluence—for those coming from rich nations, at least. And as they went back to their well off lifestyles, the demand for entertainment and the trappings of the good life increased. Boxing—anything but tools of mass destruction!—was sorely missed by fight fans all over the world. It was time to bring the ring action back.

Although the NBA sanctioned what it billed as world championship fights, the contests were held almost exclusively in the US. Also, most of the protagonists involved Americans. (The politically inclined may add: the protagonists mostly involved white Americans.) Which was why, if one was not American and he wanted to become a world champion—like Pancho Villa of the Philippines—he needed to sail away towards America and got himself lined up for a series of fights leading to the championship bout itself. For "outsiders," winning titles was thus twice harder.

As the boxing fever hit many countries (like the Central and Latin American countries, Japan, Thailand and the Philippines in Asia, Italy, Germany and France in Europe, aside of course from the UK and the US), the need to make the NBA truly global intensified. And so, in 1962, the NBA regrouped and assumed an international identity, calling itself World Boxing Association.

From its birth as NBA in 1920 until 1974, the North Americans had led WBA. After which the Latinos took over. Dr. Elias Cordova of Panama initiated what would become an uninterrupted reign by Latin Americans from 1974 up to the present, Gilberto Mendoza of Panama, the current WBA President, has been in office since 1982. Hopping from the US to Panama (1980s) and from Panama to Venezuela (1990s), the WBA headquarters went back to Panama in 2007.

As it happened anywhere in boxing (or in anything that involves mortal beings, for that matter), the WBA has not escaped from corruption allegations. The ones that became public knowledge included (1) a 1981 Sports Illustrated story where the WBA president supposedly pressured a boxing judge to favor some boxers; and (2) a year later, in 1982, Top Rank's Bob Arum was quoted in a media interview as saying that he bribed WBA officials to secure higher rankings for his fighters.

On the positive side, the WBA has maintained a continuous process of refining its policies. A more recent innovation is the award of a Super Champion status to any WBA champion who also holds titles from other sanctioning bodies (eg WBC, IBF or WBO) for the same weight division. Otherwise a WBA champion is simply recognized as a regular champion. Under this rule, the regular title for the particular weight class involved becomes vacant whenever a Super Champion emerges. Lower ranked fighters can then vie for it in a title bout.

World Boxing Council

One year after the National Boxing Association re-organized to become the World Boxing Association, its rival—the New York State Athletic Council—made itself handy in facilitating the creation of what would be called the World Boxing Council (WBC). The government of Mexico hosted an 11-country convention on February 14, 1963 with the aim of creating a sanctioning body for the sport of boxing that it claimed benefited from a genuine global mandate and constituency.

The countries that founded the WBC included the USA, Argentina, Great Britain, France, Mexico, Philippines, Panama, Chile, Peru, Venezuela and Brazil. The country representatives were Luis Spota and Professor Ramon G. Velazquez of Mexico, Onslow Fane, Bobby Naldoo and Alexander Elliot of England, Justiniano Montano of the Philippines, Piero Pini and Antonio Sciarra of Italy, Fernand Leclerc and Edouard Rabret of France and Bob Turley, Nat Fleisher, Gen. Melvin Krulewitch, George Parnassus, Anthony Petronella, Don Larsen, Emile Bruneau, all from the USA, Lazaro Kosi and Yçcaro Frusca of Argentina, and Rodrigo Sanchez of Panama, among others.

A policy innovation currently introduced by the WBC which can be viewed as resembling the aesthetic intent of WBA's Super Champion is its "Diamond Belt." This one is meant for elite champions whose title or titles were contested at an agreed catch weight.

Lawyer Rodrigo Salud of the Philippines served as its first Secretary General. Mexico's Jose Sulaiman is the current President. The WBC maintains its head office in Mexico.

International Boxing Federation

The International Boxing Federation (IBF) could be considered as a descendant of the United States Boxing Association (USBA). The USBA used to be a regional affiliate of the World Boxing Association. When the WBA convened in Puerto Rico in 1983 to elect a president, the USBA was represented by Bob Lee, its president. He ran for the WBA presidency but lost to Gilberto Mendoza.

Lee and some of his supporters in the convention left the WBA afterward and went on to organize the IBF (initially called USBA-International). The IBF put up, and currently maintains, its headquarters in New Jersey, USA.

The IBF's maiden year went largely unnoticed. By its second year, in 1984, it recognized big names like Larry Holmes, Marvelous Marvin Hagler and Aaron Pryor as IBF champions in their respective divisions. It was a masterstroke. Holmes, widely known as the most deserving among the heavyweight champion at the time, decided to relinquish his WBC belt and kept his IBF title.

This gave rise to a situation where the IBF gained some degree of acceptance from the boxing publics, gradually establishing its legitimacy as the "third" consequential sanctioning body of boxing (outside of the WBA and WBC).

Other great boxers who won IBF championship belts included Félix Trinidad (Welterweight champion from 1993 to 2000) and Ukrainian Vladimir Klitschko, the current IBF heavyweight champion.

But like the WBA and WBC at some points in their respective histories, the IBF went down once from the weight of unsavory charges. In 1999, Lee was convicted for racketeering and other crimes (like accepting bribes for better boxer rankings). He left as IBF President in shame.

Hiawatha Knight replaced Lee to become the first woman president of any boxing organization with a global constituency. Her successor, Marian Muhammad assumed the IBF presidency in 2001.

World Boxing Organization

What the IBF did in 1983 would be repeated in 1988. But while North American delegates bolted the WBA the first time, delegates from Latin America led the breakaway group the second time. The WBA was holding its annual convention in Venezuela in 1988 when businessmen from Puerto Rico and the Dominican Republic decided to do it their own way and proceeded to put up the World Boxing Organization (WBO).

In a relatively short time that the WBO has been in existence, several name fighters have won its championship belts. They included Oscar De La Hoya, Marco Antonio Barrera, Ronald "Winky" Wright, Naseem Hamed, Verno Phillips, Michael Carbajal, Johnny Tapia, Harry Simon, Jermain Taylor, Nigel Benn, Paul "Silky" Jones, Gerald McClellan, Joe Calzaghe, Steve Collins, Daniel Santos, Michael Moorer, Dariusz Michalczewski, Chris Eubank, Vitali Klitschko, Wladimir Klitschko, Chris Byrd, among others.

The WBO headquarters are based in San Juan, Puerto Rico. Francisco Varcarcel, its current president, has been in office since 1996.

International Boxing Organization

The International Boxing Organization (IBO) is another sanctioning body for professional boxing that awards world championship titles. Incorporated as a for-profit organization by John Daddono in 1992, the IBO holds offices in Florida, USA. Ed Levine currently serves as President of the IBO.

A significant contribution by IBO to boxing is the computerized system of rating boxers which it implemented in late 1990s. The system seeks to eliminate the subjective nature in which the rating process is done and thereby enhance the credibility of rankings and championships awarded to boxers.

Apparently wary of cases of dysfunctions and irregularities that tarnished the reputation of the more established sanctioning organizations, the IBO branded itself as champion of integrity and trust in boxing. It limits, as one of its integrity-enhancing measures, the grant of licenses to rigorously-selected 30 judges and 20 referees. It also vows transparency in the conduct of its business, particularly where its financial records are concerned.

Other Organizations

Although less known to the public, there are other sanctioning bodies of professional boxing. To this group belong the likes of the International Boxing Association, International Boxing Council, International Boxing Union, World Boxing Federation, World Boxing Union, among many others.

ALL ABOUT WEIGHT

In the beginning when weight classes became part of boxing, there were only two divisions: the Heavyweight and the Light(er)weight), set by the 1738 Broughton's Rules governing prize fights.

The Amateur Boxing Association brought it to 4 in 1880, by adding the Middleweight and Featherweight classes. Then the UK's Pelican Club (Pugilistic Society and London Boxing Club), which was the forerunner of the National Sporting Club, and which in turn became the British Board of Boxing Control, added one more in 1889, the Bantamweight division. This would later become flyweight, only to be modified three times later as featherweight.

When the National Sporting Club amended the Queensberry Rules in 1891 (fleshing out in more detail the rules on roles of officials, system of scoring bouts, and enabling referees to determine who won, among other things), a more or less universally-coherent attempt to define the weight classes began. By 1910, 8 weight classes became official, namely: (1) Heavyweight (176 lbs plus); (2) Cruiserweight (175 lb maximum) later called "lighter heavyweight" by the British and "light heavyweight" by the Americans; (3) Middleweight (160 lbs maximum); (4) Welterweight (147 lbs maximum); (5) Lightweight (135 lbs); (6) Featherweight (126 lbs maximum); (7) Bantamweight (118 lbs maximum); and (8) Flyweight (112 lbs max).

In 1920, the Walker Law (and as implemented by both the NBA and NYSAC) institutionalized

Diego Corrales-Jose Luis Castillo 1: Left photo shows Diego Corrales, right, pummeling Luis Castillo with both hands in the 10th round of their lightweight title match on May 5, 2005 in Mandalay Bay, Las Vegas, USA. Universally acclaimed Fight of the Year in 2005, Corrales pulled himself up from the brink of defeat to stop Castillo in that round. **Photo by Sports Illustrated.**

14 weight divisions, adding to the original list of 8 the Junior Middleweight, Junior Welterweight, Junior Lightweight, Junior Featherweight, Junior Bantamweight and Junior Flyweight.

The WBC introduced the Cruiserweight in 1979. From the original weight limit of 190-195 pounds, the WBC, WBA and IBF (in 2004) altogether fixed it to 200 pounds. In 1984, the IBF added the Super Middleweight division and, in 1987, included Straw weight or Minimum weight into its official list of weight classes.

More historical trivia on the weight divisions are on Page 39. Also presented on Page 45, in summary form, is the current configuration of the 17 weight divisions.

How Heavy Is A Few Pounds More?

A close look at the weight divisions will show that the difference in weights between divisions decrease as the division becomes lighter. For example, the difference from Cruiserweight (200 lbs) to Light Heavyweight (175 lbs) is 25 pounds. The difference narrows to 15 pounds at the next major division (Middleweight), which is pegged at 160 pounds. From Middleweight to Welterweight (147 lbs), the difference drops further to 13 pounds. Going down to the next major division, which is Lightweight (135 lbs), the difference is 12 pounds. From Lightweight to Featherweight (126 lbs), the difference continues to decrease to 9 pounds. From Featherweight down to the next major division, which is Bantamweight (118 lbs), the difference is 8 pounds. Finally, from Bantamweight to Flyweight (112 lbs), the difference shrinks even more to 6 pounds.

Why is a difference in weight seemingly more crucial at the lighter weights than at the heavier weight divisions? Sanctioning bodies and government regulating agencies are one in saying that inputs from related scientific research and ring doctors form part of the information that went into the overall safety framework for boxing, as defined, for example, in fixing weight limits for each division, or the number of rounds for which kind of bout (say title or non-title) or at what level boxers are competing.

Evander Holyfield, former heavyweight champion and future Hall of Famer, once explained that boxers who compete at the higher divisions, particularly the heavyweight division, possess power that is more or less equal even if their weights differ by several pounds (Box, page 13). What one can analyze from Holyfield's view is that at the heavier weights, the determining factor is skill (they have more or less the same power). At the lighter weights, the determining factor is power (they have more or less the same speed). Which can explain why the weight divisions at the lighter classes are crucial.

This one of many cases may further help explain it. The late Diego Corrales once backed out in 2006 from a title fight against challenger Jose Luis Castillo because the latter could not shed an excess of 4½ pounds at weigh-in. Billed as "The War To Settle The Score," the bout should have been the third fight between the two boxers. Their first fight (for WBC and WBO lightweight titles) on May 5, 2005 was a classic in non-stop action, with Castillo flooring Corrales several times in the latter rounds. But in the 10th round, Corrales—although bleeding and visibly dazed from the constant pounding he got from Castillo—stunned Castillo with a short right hook, and the latter could not recover in time to ward off a barrage of two-fisted attack from Corrales in the ensuing few seconds. Castillo lost by TKO. The way the fight was fought by both fighters was compelling enough that talk of a rematch had already started even before the fight ended.

The rematch happened 5 months later, on October 8, 2005 at Thomas & Mack Center, Las Vegas, Nevada, USA. Despite efforts to rid himself of excess poundage during weigh-in, Castillo still ended up heavier by more than 3 pounds. Corrales could have refused to fight Castillo by invoking pertinent contract provisions, such as on the ground of weight violation, but he opted to face Castillo on the next day anyway. On fight night, both fighters dished out the same brand of toe-to-toe non-stop action, like they did in their first bout. But unlike the way it ended in their first duel, Castillo this time exacted revenge, knocking Corrales out in the fourth round.

Their head-to-head match-up now even, a de-

Weight Limit	WBA	WBC	IBF	WBO
Unlimited	Heavyweight			
200lb (90.72kg)	Cruiserweight	Cruiserweight	Cruiserweight	Junior Heavyweight
175 lb (79.4 kg)	Light Heavyweight			
168 lb (76.2 kg)	Super Middleweight			
160 lb (72.6 kg)	Middleweight			
154 lb (69.9 kg)	Super Welterweight	Super Welterweight	Junior Middleweight	Junior Middleweight
147 lb (66.7 kg)	Welterweight			
140 lb (63.5 kg)	Super Lightweight	Super Lightweight	Junior Welterweight	Junior Welterweight
135 lb (61.2 kg)	Lightweight			
130 lb (59.0 kg)	Super Featherweight	Super Featherweight	Junior Lightweight	Junior Lightweight
126 lb (57.2 kg)	Featherweight			
122 lb (55.3 kg)	Super Bantamweight	Super Bantamweight	Junior Featherweight	Junior Featherweight
118 lb (53.5 kg)	Bantamweight			
115 lb (52.2 kg)	Super Flyweight	Super Flyweight	Junior Bantamweight	Junior Bantamweight
112 lb (50.8 kg)	Flyweight			
108 lb (49.0 kg)	Light Flyweight	Light Flyweight	Junior Flyweight	Junior Flyweight
105 lb (47.6 kg)	Minimumweight	Strawweight	Mini Flyweight	Mini Flyweight

ciding third bout between them not only appeared logical, it seemed that fight fans just could not get enough of Corrales and Castillo.

But Corrales refused to fight Castillo this time, saying "I have a family to support." With Corrales-Castillo 2 still freshly looming as backdrop, he was undoubtedly concerned that a few pounds more in favor of the opponent could be dangerous to his health. Making up for family welfare must have meant something to him. Four years earlier, in 2002, Corrales served 14 months of jail time for charges of beating his pregnant wife.

It turned out that Corrales didn't have much time to personally take care of his family. On May 5, 2007, or exactly 2 years after he faced Castillo in their epic first fight, Corrales died from a motorcycle accident in Las Vegas.

The Pound-for-Pound Debate

Boxing experts for years have indulged themselves in the unending debate of who is the greatest ever among the great fighters. But because it seldom happened that these great fighters faced each other owing to differences in size and the time in which they actively competed, all products of any effort to rank boxers according to their relative places in the list of all-time greats would have to remain an opinion, and therefore a potential "fodder for more debate."

Syllogism could have been useful, like: All heavyweights are KO artists; Mike Tyson is a heavyweight; therefore Mike Tyson is a KO artist. But in boxing, basic logic offers little help: Antonio Tarver lost to Bernard Hopkins; Bernard Hopkins lost to Roy Jones Jr; therefore, Antonio Tarver will lose to Roy Jones Jr? That's where the problem lies. Jones Jr, in fact, has already lost to Antonio Tarver. Not once, but twice.

Roy Jones Jr., left, out pointed WBA Heavyweight Champion **John Ruiz** (226 lbs) in 2003 to become the only former middleweight champion (160 lbs) since **Bob Fitzsimmons** (1897) to have won a heavyweight title. **Photo by Google Images.**

What seems more widely accepted is the idea that differences in terms of poundage are more crucial at lighter weights than at heavier weights. It suggests, then, that for lighter fighters to succeed in higher divisions—as shown by the likes of Roberto Duran and Manny Pacquiao—they need to hurdle tougher tests than there normally are.

THE ALL-TIME GREATS

Professional boxing had its grand moments in various eras brought about by the extra-ordinary achievements of its practitioners. Since the rise in significance of financial opportunities it offered at the turn of the 20th century, boxing has produced phenomenal athletes, and has generated quite a following throughout the world. As an example: Jack Dempsey and Gene Tunney attracted 120,557 fans in a single bout they held at the Sesquicentennial Stadium, Philadelphia, Pennsylvania, USA, on September 23, 1926. On September 12, 1951, England's Randy Turpin, after having dethroned Sugar Ray Robinson for the Middleweight crown 2 months earlier in London, staked and lost his title in a rematch before a crowd of 61,437 in New York, USA. Before defending the Junior Lightweight belt for

7 straight years in the 60s, Filipino Gabriel "Flash" Elorde won his title from Harold Gomes in front of some 26,000 paying fans at the Araneta Coliseum (same site of Ali-Frazier 3), Quezon City, Philippines. And, fast forward, get this: more than 2.15 million American boxing fans paid an average of $56 dollars for pay-per-view access to the Oscar De La Hoya-Floyd Mayweather match in Las Vegas, Nevada, USA on May 5, 2007. Millions more with online access and satellite links watched the fight throughout the world.

Except for the periods in which the countries of the world were at war, boxing rocked and rolled, as it were, alongside the pages of human history. Glimpses of great moments in boxing were forever etched in the memory of hard core fight fans. It is fitting, now as it was then, to once more recognize the fighters who shined the brightest during their time, bringing prestige to the craft with their discipline, hard work, courage and God-given athletic abilities.

FIGHTERS OF THE DECADE
1910s-1920s

BoxRec Boxing Encyclopedia wrote that "Jack Dempsey changed the sport of boxing from a slow, defense-minded contest of single punches and frequent holding into an exciting, aggressive battle of furious combinations and blazing knockouts." But his life outside the ring gave him a bad press. Widely regarded by many as "a thug wallowing in immorality and brutality," fans loved to hate him. And yet when Gene Tunney dethroned him in 1926 after a 7-year reign, fans ironically began to admire him. Tunney was the epitome of an intelligent and scientific boxer, and they found him boring to watch. They missed Jack's "ultra-masculine charisma and slugger's brawn." In his time, nobody packed the crowds in quite like Dempsey did.

Still, when the scribes minted the term "pound-for-pound" during this period, it was not because of Dempsey. It was because of Benny Leonard, who reigned as Lightweight Champion from May 1917 to January 1925. Boxing experts argued that Leonard at this time was the best, pound for pound. They also made mention of Harry Greb, a Middleweight Champion from 1923 to 1926. Greb has incredibly beaten heavier opponents in the light heavyweight and heavyweight divisions. He held the distinction of being the only fighter to ever beat Gene Tunney.

1930's

Henry Armstrong rocked the boxing world in 1937 and 1938, generating after-shocks that would continue to be felt until now. At a time when there were only 8 weight divisions, he won the featherweight, welterweight and lightweight titles in succession within a period of 10 months (from October 1937 to August 1938). Thus Armstrong would go down in boxing history as the only fighter ever to hold 3 world titles in 3 different divisions all at the same time.

Also at this time, Heavyweight Champion Joe Louis started a terrific run and would continue to dominate the opposition towards the latter part of the 40s. Earlier in the decade, Barney Ross stamped his class in the lightweight and welterweight divisions, besting fellow all-time great Tony Canzoneri, among others, twice.

1940's

World War 2 momentarily halted ring action except on very few occasions. Joe Louis kept his title despite being out of ring action due to his military service, and when he did return in 1946, he defended it 5 more times until Ezzard Charles defeated him in 1950.

At the lighter divisions, Featherweight Champion Willie Pep was making it hard for anyone not to notice him. He won 229 of his 241 fights, and showing, in the process, his opponents the finer points of defense in boxing.

Towards the late 1940's, the welterweight division had ran out of warm bodies that were capable of putting up a decent competition against a rising star named Sugar Ray Robinson.

1950's

Sugar Ray Robinson remained lord of welterweights and was, by now, the newest darling of boxing. He reminded boxing historians of Benny Leonard, Henry Armstrong, Willie Pep and all the great boxers of the lighter weight divisions before him. The only difference with them, it seemed, was that he was better. When he annexed the middleweight crown early in the decade and outclassed the best middle-weights afterward, the term "pound-for-pound" champion that briefly emerged during Leonard's era was back, and it was firmly associated with Robinson. Fans found him so good that beating him—which the likes of Carmen Basilio and Gene Fullmer did when Robinson was apparently past his prime—meant earning for themselves an exalted place in the all-time greats list.

1960's

Cassius Clay became Muhammad Ali on the same night he wrested the heavyweight crown from Sonny Liston in 1964. Producing spectacular wins inside the ring and creating political drama outside of it made Ali the most recognized—and probably adored—athlete in this era.

The lighter weight divisions produced more exciting fighters in Bantamweight Champion Edre Jofre, his conqueror Fighting Harada of Japan, Junior Lightweight King Gabriel "Flash" Elorde, and Lightweight Champion Carlos Ortiz.

1970's

In no time was there such a bumper harvest, so to speak, of talent in the heavyweight division as in this period. Ali, Joe Frazier and George Foreman were not only former Olympic stars, all of them were also undefeated challengers when they all won the heavyweight championship. Frazier grabbed the title vacated by Ali (who preferred to be in jail rather than in military service during the American-Vietnam war in the 60s and 70s). Frazier yielded it to Foreman via a second round KO loss. Ali recaptured his title from Foreman after besting the latter in 8 rounds.

Elsewhere, Carlos Monzon rose to the Middleweight throne in 1970 and ran out of abled opponents in that division until he retired in 1977. Experts viewed him as the pound for pound champion in this era—that is, until Roberto Duran came along.

1980's

Like what Monzon did in the middleweight class, Duran thrashed all comers in the lightweight division. He eventually invaded the talent-laden welterweight and middleweight divisions. He won the welterweight championship from Sugar Ray Leonard in their first encounter (1980), only to relinquish it back to Leonard in their return bout. Leonard did not only bested Duran in their 3-bout match-up, he beat Hall of Famer Thomas Hearns and decisioned Middleweight all-time great Marvin Marvelous Hagler, among many other who's who in boxing.

1990's

Julio Cesar Chavez, Pernell Whitaker, Oscar De La Hoya and Roy Jones Junior dominated their respective divisions during this period. Although Chavez, Whitaker and De La Hoya crossed paths at some points in their careers, one would be off his peak in relation to the other. The outcomes of their personal match-ups could therefore hardly be a measure of who was superior to whom. Jones? He rocked (for a time, that is).

2000's

Jones and De La Hoya eventually shared the limelight to relative newcomers Shane Mosley, Bernard Hopkins and Floyd Mayweather. All of them would be accorded with the pound for pound title at certain points in their careers, with Mayweather considered as the best until he retired in 2007. Meanwhile, Manny Pacquiao scaled the higher weight divisions in blitzkrieg fashion. Starting as a flyweight champion in 1998, he won the bantamweight crown in 2001, the featherweight top honor in 2003, the super featherweight belt in March 2008, the lightweight championship in July 2008, the light welterweight trophy in May 2009, and the welterweight 6 months later. In December 2008, he faced De La Hoya also at 147 pounds and mauled him in 7 rounds. Experts conceded that the kind of ascent he did had never been done by any fighter before.

Meantime, Mayweather decided to rejoin the fray, celebrating his return to ring action with a convincing decision win over Juan Manuel Marquez in September 2009. A month later, Pacquiao himself solidified his unique status among the world's greatest boxers by becoming the only fighter to have won world titles in 7 weight divisions when he defeated Miguel Cotto for the latter's welterweight crown. The result of both bouts had left the boxing world itching to

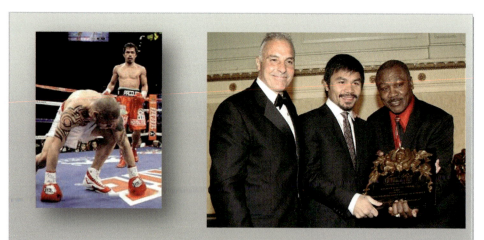

ONE OF A KIND. After beating Welterweight Champion **Miguel Cotto** (left) on November 13, 2009, **Manny Pacquiao** (left) became the only fighter, past or present, to have won world titles in 7 different weight divisions. In scaling his way to the top, **Pacquiao** rose from Flyweight (112 pounds) to Welterweight (147 pounds), knocking down a total of 9 weight divisions. Right photo shows Manny Pacquiao receiving from **Smokin' Joe Frazier** the **Boxing Writers Association of America (BWAA)** "Fighter of the Decade Award" on June 4, 2010 at Roosevelt Hotel, New York, USA. During the occasion, Pacquiao also received for the 3rd consecutive time the BWAA "Fighter of the Year Award". **Photo by Sports Illustrated and BWAA.**

see if Mayweather can reclaim his pound for pound title from Pacquiao through a ring battle.

THE ALL-TIME GREAT LISTS

There can be as many lists of who are the greatest fighters of all time as there are fans and stakeholders of boxing. But, as has been mentioned, such lists are products of opinion. Which means one list can only be as good as the other. As Andrew Eisele of About.com notes on the Ring Magazine's list of 80 best fighters of the previous 80 years which came out in 2002, "the entirely subjective nature of any list comparing fighters across different weight categories and different eras is bound to be fodder for debate…"

The Lists' Rankings

We are presenting here five lists of the greatest fighters of all time. The lists are made by the ESPN, Associated Press, Ring Magazine and the Greatest Ever. The Ring Magazine list comprises two separate lists, one is the 80 best fighters of the previous 80 years released in 2002, as mentioned above, and the other is its annual pound-for-pound list, which first came out in 1989. The Ring Magazine's pound-for-pound list is important, because the other lists, except the Greatest Ever, have been published prior to the period covered by the P4P list.

The choice itself of the ESPN, AP, Ring Magazine and The Greatest Ever lists can be tagged as subjective. Except to say that these list-makers had been around long enough to know what they are talking about, there is nothing much we can do by way of defending that choice, because that's what it truly is—subjective. Again, the Greatest Ever could be an exception. A relative newcomer, its list reportedly represents the collective opinion of .5 million respondents.

One may notice that three lists stopped at ten, the pound-for-pound list at 8, and The Greatest Ever at 3. Except for the pound-for-pound and The Greatest Ever lists, the 3 other lists did not stop there. This book did. But it will try to fully cover them in the next edition, hopefully.

Presented below are the top ten greatest boxers of all time, according to the ESPN, AP, Ring Magazine, and The Greatest Ever.

The ESPN top ten boxers of all time:

1. Sugar Ray Robinson	2. Muhammad Ali
3. Henry Armstrong	4. Joe Louis
5. Willie Pep	6. Roberto Duran
7. Benny Leonard	8. Jack Johnson
9. Jack Dempsey	10. Sam Langford

The Associated Press top ten boxers of all time:

1. Sugar Ray Robinson	2. Muhammad Ali
3. Henry Armstrong	4. Joe Louis
5. Willie Pep	6. Jack Dempsey
7. Roberto Duran	8. Benny Leonard
9. Billy Conn	10. Harry Greb

The Ring Magazine top ten boxers in the last 80 years:

1. Sugar Ray Robinson	2. Henry Armstrong
3. Muhammad Ali	4. Joe Louis
5. Roberto Duran	6. Willie Pep
7. Harry Greb	8. Benny Leonard
9. Sugar Ray Leonard	10. Pernnell Whitaker

The Greatest Ever (2009):

1. Sugar Ray Robinson   2. Manny Pacquiao

3. Muhammad Ali

The Ring Magazine Pound-For-Pound Champions (annual list started in 1989):

1. Mike Tyson (1989)

2. Julio Cesar Chavez (1990-1992)

3. Roy Jones (1996, 1999, 2003)

4. Oscar De La Hoya (1997-1998)

5. Shane Mosley (2000-2001)

6. Bernard Hopkins (2002, 2004)

7. Floyd Mayweather (2005-2007)

8. Manny Pacquiao (2008-2010)

The elite boxers who are in at least one of the 4 lists and the pound-for-pound list above are:

1. Sugar Ray Robinson	2. Muhammad Ali
3. Henry Armstrong	4. Joe Louis
5. Willie Pep	6. Roberto Duran
7. Benny Leonard	8. Jack Johnson
9. Jack Dempsey	10. Sam Langford
11. Billy Conn	12. Harry Greb
13. Sugar Ray Leonard	14. Pernnel Whitaker
15. Mike Tyson	16. J Cesar Chavez
17. Roy Jones Jr	18. Oscar De La Hoya
19. Shane Mosely	20. Bernard Hopkins
21. Floyd Mayweather	22. Manny Pacquiao

Again, it must be mentioned at this point that the three lists did not stop at ten. It is only here, and for purposes of this book, that the lists did not go beyond number ten. The Ring Magazine's pound for pound list is kind of exception, since all pound for pound champions who made it to the top of that list since 1989 are included here.

Having said that, we shall now subject these top 22 fighters to further analysis and come up with a final overall ranking.

Sugar Ray Robinson

"Sugar" Ray Robinson's resume speaks for itself. A hundred seventy-three wins out of 200 fistic contests in a pro career that span 23 years.

But what separates Robinson from ordinary fighters is seen not only by way of looking at the long list of his conquests, but also at the way he conquered his opponents. His technique, boxing skills and ring generalship were simply too advanced—even for his time—to be ignored. To his credit must also go true grit and courage by which he tested his limits inside the ring, as well as an infinite supply of passion for the sport.

Robinson had a natural flair for boxing. Almost always being able to find a way to win, his boxing style was a study of how fighters should respond to any given situation presented to them by their opponents. He was quick with both hands and feet. He was impeccable with his jabs. He loads, unloads and reloads at the perfect time. He was fearless in mixing up with brawlers. He can throw bombs and knock people out double his size.

And probably the most eloquent expression of his greatness could be found in the way future boxers who would be legends themselves have made his brand of boxing their own.

Muhammad Ali and Sugar Ray Leonard, for example, had displayed boxing wizardry that reminded the fans of Robinson. Applying excellent footwork to launch their attack, they ex-

ued to be active until he was 51 years old (like appearing in exhibition bouts), he retired from professional boxing at age 44.

Muhammad Ali

Cassius Clay did not need a publicist. He was his own best endorser. Calling himself "The Greatest" and "The Prettiest" of all time, he liked to be in front of flicking camera lenses.

Even on his first televised amateur bout when he was around 15, he knocked on his neighbors' doors to make sure people got to watch him perform as a boxer.

And the interesting part about Clay was that he lived up to his own hype. Boxing night after boxing night, he did his job almost always with exclamation marks, and fans conceded that he was good as advertised.

Born To Be A Star

After having been crowned as the Light Heavyweight champion in the 1960 Rome Olympics,

PROFILE SUMMARY			
Name:	Muhammad Ali	Professional Career Highlights	
Alias:	Louisville Lip / The Greatest	Total Fights	61
Birth Name:	Cassius Marcellus Clay	Wins	56
Birth Place:	Louisville, Kentucky, USA	Winning Percentage	91.80
Birth Date:	17 January 1942	Losses	5
Death Date:	NA	Draws	0
Nationality:	United States	NCs/Disqualifications	0
Residence:	Louisville, Kentucky, USA	KOs	37
Stance:	Orthodox	KO Percentage	66.07
Height:	6'3" / 191 cm	Percentage of Quality Wins	94.92
Reach:	80" / 203 cm	Years Active	19

World Titles in Different Weight Divisions					
DIVISION	TOTAL DIV TITLES	FROM		TO	
		Month	Year	Month	Year
WBA/WBC Heavyweight	1	Feb	1964	May	1967
WBA/WBC Heavyweight		Oct	1974	Feb	1978
WBA Heavyweight		Sep	1978	Sep	1979
TOTAL	1				

THRILLA IN MANILA. Muhammad Ali and **Joe Frazier** waged three fierce ring battles against each other. In Ali-Frazier 3, (shown in photo, Sep 1975, Philippines), Ali admitted to media after the bout (which he won by TKO in the 14th round) that the contest left him battered, exhausted, and almost close to dying. **Photo by Sports Illustrated.**

Clay would broke himself into the limelight as he outclassed his opponents in the professional ranks. He splattered media interviews with rhymes, like "They all fall / In the round I call."

By 1963, big names like Archie Moore, Henry Cooper and the upcoming Billy Daniels had been caught in a whirlwind that Clay was.

At 24 his numbers were already quite impressive: 19 straight wins, 16 of them by knockout, along with probably thousands of clowning antics before the media. And yet, as he faced Sonny Liston for the heavyweight crown on February 25, 1964, boxing fans still hardly saw him as a serious contender. And Liston had a lot to do with it. Like Mike Tyson who would succeed him a couple of decades later, Liston evoked fear in his opponents that they looked defeated even before a fight started. On two occasions Liston had knocked out Floyd Patterson (from whom he wrested his title) in the first round.

But Clay would have none of Liston's intimidating credentials. Instead, he vowed to finish Liston inside 7 rounds. And he delivered. In an instant, he converted thousands of unbelievers. Eyes followed him wherever he went. He was, by now, a star.

Celebrity With A Cause?

It turned out his playful mien was cover for a serious racial and political advocacy that raged at the core of his being. On the night he won the heavyweight title, he announced his conversion to Islam. He called himself a Black Muslim, and answered back only when called by his new name—Muhammad Ali.

In time he would defy America. He slammed the American-Vietnam war in the 60s and refused, on religious grounds, to be enlisted for military service in that war.

Times were tough for his otherwise booming boxing career. His social beliefs were getting in the way of his rise in stock as a celebrity, like humps on the road to greatness. That was how his fans saw it. On the other hand, fame helped get his message across. This was how Ali saw it. In any case, he lost his heavyweight crown in 1967 due to the political conflicts he created.

It took him three years to navigate back from the fringes to the boxing mainstream. On March 8, 1971, he faced a future arch-rival in Smoking Joe Frazier in a bout dubbed as "Battle of Champions" at the Madison Square Garden, New York, USA. Also an Olympic Gold medalist and so far unbeaten as a professional fighter like himself, Frazier on fight night bobbed and weaved, braving a continuous assault of jabs and straights from Ali. Frazier's hope was in landing one solid left hook of his own; and he succeeded in the 11th round. Ali crashed backwards against the ropes before finally hitting the canvass, like a chopper that lost three of its four blades. Frazier won by decision.

Three years later Ali and Frazier would clash again (1974), and again (1975), with Ali coming out victorious on both occasions.

Ali recaptured his crown when he dethroned George Foreman on October 30, 1974 in Kinshasha, Zaire (now Congo). After seeing his defeat to Frazier, who had KOd 23 of his 27 victims (no loss) at the time they first met, fight fans were back at not taking Ali too seriously. Apparently for good reasons. Foreman had, 2 years earlier, dethroned Frazier with a single blow to the head in the second round of their championship bout. He made short work of most other guys too. Coming to the Ali fight, Foreman had an unblemished record of 40 wins, 37 of which inside the distance.

And yet, as in the Liston fight, Ali silenced the doubters. He used the ropes to cushion the impact of Foreman's thunderous assault. It was "rope a dope," another grain of technique brought to boxing by Ali, said the boxing scholars. Sensing the dissipation of energy in his foe, Ali went for the kill in the 8th round. Lefts and rights from all directions landed on Foreman's face. Foreman fell; his feet almost touching the roof of the boxing arena as his back settled on the floor of the ring. He appeared relieved, nevertheless, when the referee counted him out to end the fight.

Ali reigned for 4 more years before a 12-round decision loss to the upset-minded Leon Spinks dislodged him from his perch. Although a former Olympic champion himself like his predecessors, boxing experts did not give Spinks much of a chance against the two-time undisputed heavyweight champion, owing largely to his relative inexperience. He fought a total of only 7 times (6 wins and a draw) before he faced Ali.

Ali recaptured his title (WBA side only; the WBC stripped Spinks of his title when he opted to fight Ali instead of Ken Norton, its top challenger) for the third time when he beat Spinks in

PROFILE SUMMARY			
Name:	Henry Armstrong	Professional Career Highlights	
Alias:	Homicide Hank	Total Fights	180
Birth Name:	Henry Melody Jackson	Wins	149
Birth Place:	St. Louis, MO	Winning Percentage	82.78
Birth Date:	12 December 1912	Losses	21
Death Date:	23 October 1988	Draws	10
Nationality:	United States	NCs/Disqualifications	0
Residence:	LA, California, USA	KOs	101
Stance:	Orthodox	KO Percentage	67.79
Height:	5'5½" / 180 cm	Percentage of Quality Wins	82.84
Reach:	67" / 170 cm	Years Active	13

World Titles in Different Weight Divisions					
DIVISION	TOTAL DIV TITLES	FROM		TO	
		Month	Year	Month	Year
Featherweight	1	Oct	1937	Sep	1938
Welterweight	1	May	1938	Oct	1940
Lightweight	1	Aug	1938	Aug	1939
TOTAL	3				

Henry Armstrong in ring action (left) and a victory pose (right). **Photos by Photobucket.com.**

their return bout on September 15, 1978 (7 months after their first fight).

Ali retired after the second Spinks fight, only to return 2 years later. He lost 2 more times before finally retiring for good, first to Larry Holmes, then to Trevor Berbick.

Now 67, he lives a modest life in Berrien Springs, Michigan, USA, with his family.

Henry Armstrong

Aspiring and average boxers may do well to draw inspiration from Henry Armstrong.

Early in his career, Armstrong hardly made an impression he would go on to become one of the world's greatest fighters. He had, well, an average start: 4 losses and 5 draws in his first 23 fights. His next 21 bouts were equally unimpressive, again losing 4 times and drawing once. By this time, he had compiled a 30-8-6 win-loss-draw record in 44 professional fights.

But after turning 24 in 1936, he started a dramatic run that would see him chalk up 41 straight wins in 3 years, including 28 wins in 1937 alone. He opened that year with a third-round knockout of Rodolfo Casanova on New Year's Day. After that he fought an average of 2.3 fights per month.

On October 29, 1937, he challenged Petey Sarron for the World Featherweight crown. He knocked out Sarron in 6 rounds and began to establish a boxing record that would remain intact until now (2009). Manny Pacquiao may have matched that feat, except that Pacquiao carved a niche for himself with slightly different dimensions.

Armstrong fought 14 more times before challenging Welterweight Champion Barney Ross on May 31, 1938. From featherweight (126 lbs), he jumped over the lightweight division (135 lbs), to face Ross at welterweight (147 lbs). At weigh in, Armstrong was lighter by 8.5 lbs at 133.5 lbs than Ross, who came in at 142 lbs.

By no means a so-so champion, Ross had a 74-3-3 win-loss-draw record when he faced Armstrong. He would eventually rank 21st in Ring Magazine's 2002 list of 80 best fighters of the last 80 years. He defeated Tony Canzoneri (No. 34 in the Ring list) twice, among other elite fighters.

But when they clashed, Armstrong dominated the heftier Ross throughout their 15-round bout. The 3 judges unanimously (12-2, 11-2, and 10-4) awarded the fight in his favor.

Maintaining his weight at 134 lbs, Armstrong returned to the ring 2½ months later to challenge Lou Ambers for the latter's lightweight crown. Like Ross, Ambers had an outstanding 75-5-7 win-loss-draw ring record, and undefeated in his last 6 fights.

During the fight itself (August 17, 1938 at Madison Square Garden, New York, USA), George Blake, on his last assignment as referee, penalized Armstrong repeatedly and awarded 4 rounds to Ambers. Armstrong, however, managed to win the bout by split decision.

Armstrong thus captured world titles in 3 weight divisions within a period of 10 months, and held them simultaneously. The feat was so extra-ordinary that it prompted the NBA to revise its rules to the effect that no champion would be allowed to hold more than one title simultaneously.

He almost rocked history books even more by trying to wrest the middleweight title (recognized by the State of California) from Filipino Ceferino Garcia. But he failed in that attempt as the bout ended in a draw. Some fans, however, felt that he should have won it.

Armstrong started his career at 19 and retired at 33.

Joe Louis

"Twenty-five consecutive title defenses. A world record. Twelve consecutive years as a world champion. Another world record. Three consecutive first-round knockouts in title defenses. Ten victories over world champions. Only one loss in his first sixty-two fights. Any way one looks at it, Joe Louis is an all-time great in the sport of boxing and a deserving hall-of-famer. But the legacy and importance of Louis exists beyond the realm of statistics. In an era when blacks were shut out of most opportunities for social equality or upward mobility, Louis succeeded in gaining the richest prize in sports, opening doors and minds like no other athlete before him. His overwhelming abilities and skills inside the ropes got him to the championship, but his sportsmanship and soft-spoken dignity made him an idol to millions. In his private life, Louis was far from a role model, but in public he was a symbol of values larger than himself. Americans

PROFILE SUMMARY

Name:	Joe Louis	Professional Career Highlights	
Alias:	The Brown Bomber	Total Fights	69
Birth Name:	Joseph Louis Barrow	Wins	66
Birth Place:	LaFayette, Alabama, United States	Winning Percentage	95.65
Birth Date:	13 May 1914	Losses	3
Death Date:	12 April 1981	Draws	0
Nationality:	United States	NCs/Disqualifications	0
Residence:	Detroit, Michigan, United States	KOs	52
Stance:	Orthodox	KO Percentage	78.79
Height:	6'2" / 188 cm	Percentage of Quality Wins	95.31
Reach:	76" / 193 cm	Years Active	14

World Titles in Different Weight Divisions

DIVISION	TOTAL DIV TITLES	FROM		TO	
		Month	Year	Month	Year
Heavyweight	1	Jun	1937	Dec	1942
Note: Joe Louis was in military service from 1943 to 1945.		Jun	1946	Sep	1950
TOTAL	1				

Joe Louis lost by KO to **Max Schmeling** in a politically-charged and highly anticipated 1936 fight. Two years later, in 1938, **Louis** returned the favor by knocking out **Schmeling** (right). **Photos by Google Images.**

of all colors, sexes, and creeds saw in him the ideals of freedom, competition, and patriotism that made him the perfect symbol of national pride during the troubled years of the Great Depression and then World War II. He may have been the greatest heavyweight in history, but much more importantly, he was a hero to an entire generation."

With that paragraph, BoxRec Boxing Encyclopedia summarizes Joe Louis' life and boxing career.

Louis toiled at an early age to help his big family earn money. His parents were sharecroppers in Alabama before they decided to relocate to Detroit, Michigan, assumably in search of better income opportunities. Louis would later reveal that delivering ice blocks—one of the odd jobs he took as a youngster—up several stairs in tenement buildings helped build his muscles and boost his stamina.

But his mother might have wished Joe to become a musician instead of a boxer. Joe himself had no inkling he would one day be wearing gloves and become the world's most feared puncher in his time, until one of his friends, Thurston McKinney, an amateur boxer, introduced him to the sport. It was on McKinney's prodding that Joe paid for boxing lessons with the money his mom gave him for piano lessons.

In 1934, at age 20, Louis would become an out-standing amateur boxer himself. He won the Amateur Athletic Union's Light Heavyweight Championship in that year. Soon after this he turned professional.

Louis had a rousing start in the pro ranks: 21 straight wins (18 by KO) in less than 2 years. The casualties included the Italian Primo Carnera, who outweighed him by at least 64 lbs. By 1936, his handlers had positioned him for the big time.

Louis faced Max Schmeling in an elimination bout for the heavyweight belt on June 19, 1936 at the Yankee Stadium, New York, USA. A former heavyweight champion himself, Schmeling bucked the odds and the fearsome reputation Louis brought with him inside the ring. Counter-punching efficiently, Schmeling had Louis in trouble most of the time until the bout ended in the 12th round. Louis lost by KO and dashed his championship dreams away.

But he came back—and quickly. He grabbed 7 straight wins (6 by KO) in 8 months after tasting his first defeat. He earned another shot at the title. Due to the political tensions hounding Schmeling's country—Germany—at the time, he failed to challenge Jim Braddock, the champion. Soon, on June 22, 1937, Louis found himself contending for Braddock's title. He knocked out the champion, won the title, and would go on to defend it 25 times in succession for 12 years. His title defenses included one that avenged his only loss so far, knocking out Schmeling in Round 1.

He enlisted for the military service during the Second World War, and was allowed to keep his boxing title while he was on military duty. He returned to ring action in 1946 and defended his title 4 more times. Ezzard Charles ended his reign in 1950. A KO loss to Rocky Marciano in 1951 pushed him to retirement.

With a boxing style that—reminiscent of Jack Dempsey—entertained the paying fans, he was easily one of the richest athletes in his time. He soon dissipated most of his earnings, however. At some point later in his life, he went broke and had to beg from family and friends to survive.

Willie Pep

When it came to "hit and don't get hit" approach to boxing, Willie Pep had no equal. That was how he earned his "Will o' the Wisp" alias. And that, essentially, was how he won 95 percent of his career fights. It must be remembered that boxing rules adopted since 1929 recognized the value of defense in boxing. The rules stated, among other things, that

"Defensive work is relatively important and points should be given for cleverly avoiding or blocking a blow."

After turning professional in 1940 at age 18, Pep stormed to 63 straight wins. That win streak included the Featherweight title bout against Chalky Wright on November 20, 1943.

After losing a non-title bout against Sammy Angott in 1943, Pep charged back with another 73 straight wins in 5 years (from 1943 to 1948), halted only by a solitary draw in 1945 against Jimmy McAllister.

From his pro debut in July 25, 1940 until 1948, Pep had already fought 138 times—winning all of them except on three occasions (2 losses and 1 draw)—for an average of 23 fights in a year.

Pep was a two-time featherweight champion. He held the title from 1943 to 1948, and then from

PROFILE SUMMARY				
Name:	Willie Pep	Professional Career Highlights		
Alias:	Will o' the Wisp	Total Fights		241
Birth Name:	Gugliermo Papaleo	Wins		229
Birth Place:	Connecticut, United States	Winning Percentage		95.02
Birth Date:	19 September 1922	Losses		11
Death Date:	23 November 2006	Draws		1
Nationality:	United States	NCs/Disqualifications		0
Residence:	Rocky Hill, Connecticut, USA	KOs		70
Stance:	Orthodox	KO Percentage		30.57
Height:	5'5" / 165 cm	Percentage of Quality Wins		92.90
Reach:	68" / 173 cm	Years Active		22
World Titles in Different Weight Divisions				
DIVISION	TOTAL DIV TITLES	FROM		TO
		Month	Year	Month	Year
Featherweight	1	Nov	1943	Oct	1948
	2		1949	Sep	1950
TOTAL	1				

The Master of Defense on the Offensive. Right photo shows **Wellie Pep** on the attack against **Sandy Saddler** (right). Pep and Saddler met 4 times—the score stood at 3-1 in Saddler's favor. **Photos by Google Images.**

1949 to 1950. During the more than six years that he was champion, he defended his crown against the best fighters in the division during this period.

Aside from Wright, he has fought and outclassed Sal Bartolo, Phil Terranova, Eddie Compo, Charley Riley, and Ray Famechon, among others. But Pep had a Waterloo in Sandy Saddler. The first time he lost his title, it was to Saddler. He regained it though in a rematch some 5 months later. In the third of what would become a 4-bout match-up, Pep lost the championship again to Saddler. In 1951, both great fighters met again inside the ring. The championship was at stake and Pep was out to reclaim it. But Saddler was emphatic in his defense, imposing his mastery over Pep with a ninth-round knockout win.

Pep was active as a prizefighter for 11 more years after losing his crown. He remained competitive for most of these years, although most of his 11

PROFILE SUMMARY

Name:	Roberto Duran	Professional Career Highlights	
Alias:	Manos de Piedra / El Cholo	Total Fights	119
Birth Name:	Roberto Duran Samaniego	Wins	103
Birth Place:	El Chorillo, Panama	Winning Percentage	86.55
Birth Date:	16 June 1951	Losses	16
Death Date:	NA	Draws	0
Nationality:	Panama	NCs/Disqualifications	0
Residence:	Panama City, Panama	KOs	70
Stance:	Orthodox	KO Percentage	67.96
Height:	5'7" / 170 cm	Percentage of Quality Wins	80.72
Reach:	66" / 168 cm	Years Active	31

World Titles in Different Weight Divisions

DIVISION	TOTAL DIV TITLES	FROM		TO	
		Month	Year	Month	Year
WBA Lightweight	1	Jun	1972	Jan	1979
WBC Welterweight	1	Jun	1980	Nov	1980
WBA Light Middleweight	1	Jun	1983	Jan	1984
WBC Middleweight	1	Feb	1989	Jan	1990
Note: WBC Lightweight Champion from Jan 1978 to Jan 1979					
TOTAL	4				

 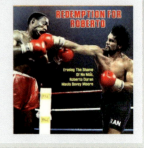

DARING THE ODDS. Before **Manny Pacquiao** demolished the weight divisions, **Roberto Duran** conquered the heights of prizefighting from Bantamweight to Super Middleweight. Right photo shows Duran tagging Davey Moore with a right en route to a TKO win on June 16, 1983. **Photos by Google Images.**

career losses happened during this span of time.

He contemplated retirement in 1959 and did not see ring action until 1965. He celebrated his return to boxing with 9 straight wins in 1965. But time had slowed him down and, unlike in his early years as a boxer, could not keep one more unbeaten streak much longer. On March 16, 1966, he battled and lost to Calvin Woodland by unanimous decision in 6 rounds. That would be his last fight. After 241 bouts in 22 years as a prizefighter, Pep retired for good.

He remained actively involved in the sport, however. After he retired from boxing, Pep tried his hand as a boxing referee. He also became the Deputy Commissioner for Boxing of Connecticut.

Roberto Duran

Legend has it that Roberto Duran swam across rivers in his hometown to steal mangoes at the other side. It was his way of ensuring that he would find himself involved in fisticuffs.

The local police could only shake their heads as they ran out of supplies updating the Duran files and trying to contain the youngster, until they thought of how such a hyper-active fetish for mayhem could be put to good use.

They brought him to a boxing gym. And the rest was history: The kid who loved to fight would

PROFILE SUMMARY				
Name:	Benny Leonard	Professional Career Highlights		
Alias:		Total Fights			217
Birth Name:	Benjamin Leiner	Wins			183
Birth Place:	East Side, New York, NY, USA	Winning Percentage			84.33
Birth Date:	17 April 1896	Losses			19
Death Date:	18 April 1947	Draws			11
Nationality:	United States	NCs/Disqualifications			4
Residence:	New York, NY, USA	KOs			70
Stance:	Orthodox	KO Percentage			38.25
Height:	5'5" / 165 cm	Percentage of Quality Wins			83.33
Reach:	69" / 175 cm	Years Active			16
World Titles in Different Weight Divisions				
DIVISION	TOTAL DIV TITLES	FROM		TO	
		Month	Year	Month	Year
Lightweight	1	May	1917	Jan	1925
TOTAL	1				

Benny Leonard, whose ring generalship inspired boxing writers in the early twenties to mint the term "pound for pound champion" ruled the lightweight division from 1917 to 1925. Right photo shows Benny Leonard matched up against Rocky Kansas in 1922. **Photos by Google Images.**

one day become one of the greatest fighters who ever lived.

He had yet to turn 17 when, on February 23, 1968, he took prizefighting as his life-long occupation. His first opponent as a professional fighter was Carlos Mendoza, whom he defeated by unanimous decision in 4 rounds.

If Duran's first few fights were any indication, his boxing career was no doubt headed to something great, and the prizefighter to stardom.

All but 4 of his first 31 fights ended in either KO or TKO.

Esteban de Jesus halted Duran's run at 32, losing to him by unanimous decision in 10 rounds. De Jesus floored Duran in the first round, and after that the bout was a breathtaking display of vicious give and take from beginning to end.

Duran and de Jesus would clash 3 more times after that. As in the first, the two locked horns in the middle of the ring, with either one unwilling to yield an inch of space to the other. But Duran was just too much class. He knocked out de Jesus in the 11th of the second bout, and in the 12th in the third and last bout.

Fighting mostly in his hometown Panama early in his career, Duran brought his brand of boxing to the United States and to the world in a 1971 fight against Benny Huertas at the Madison Square

PROFILE SUMMARY

Name:	Jack Johnson	**Professional Career Highlights**	
Alias:	Galveston Giant	Total Fights	101
Birth Name:	John Arthur Johnson	Wins	73
Birth Place:	Galveston, Texas, USA	Winning Percentage	72.28
Birth Date:	31 March 1878	Losses	13
Death Date:	10 June 1946	Draws	10
Nationality:	United States	NCs/Disqualifications	5
Residence:	Raleigh, North Carolina, USA	KOs	40
Stance:	Orthodox	KO Percentage	54.79
Height:	6'1" / 187 cm	Percentage of Quality Wins	68.92
Reach:	74" / 188 cm	Years Active	23

World Titles in Different Weight Divisions

DIVISION	TOTAL DIV TITLES	FROM		TO	
		Month	Year	Month	Year
Heavyweight	1	Dec	1908	Apr	1915
TOTAL	1				

Jack Johnson's reign as heavyweight champion (1908-1915) sparked contentious issues largely because, one, of his being black and, two, of his "arrogant" defiance against social norms that accord low regard to people of his color. Right photo shows **Black Jack** knocking out **Stanley Ketchel** on October 16, 1909. **Photos by Google Images.**

Garden in New York. Boxing fans who saw him for the first time wondered if what was before them was at all human. He had fire in his eyes that encouraged an opponent to seek out the nearest exit. And when the bell rang, he was like a bomb packaged in human form, ready to detonate anytime inside the ring.

Ring action had barely turned on the heat when Duran exploded, knocking out Huertas in the first round.

That fight alerted the boxing world of his arrival, and from then on boxing fans wanted to see more of Duran. And yes, he went on to awe the fans in more than a hundred exacting ring battles. He competed for 31 years (the longest in boxing history) in a career that spanned 5 decades (also a record). No one knew how much longer he planned to continue fighting. What many people would later know was that a life-threatening car accident in Argentina in 2001 forced him out of the ring, never to compete again. The decision may have been made with reluctance, but he nevertheless ended his boxing career with a 103-16 win-loss record.

Duran fought the who's who of boxing in his time and beyond: Ken Buchanan, Sugar Ray Leonard (winning once but losing twice), Iran Barkley, Davey Moore, Marvin Hagler, Thomas Hearns, among many others. Anywhere and whomever he fought he brought to the ring an almost unique menu of boxing, one that would not be his if it did not consist of ferocious and relentless attack.

At 51, Duran was the same 15-year-old kid who loved to fight, the same thrill-seeker who forced the police to dump him to the gym. He did become fight shy 2 decades earlier. Duran was 29 when Leonard, in their rematch, boxed him rather than engaged him in a brawl. He would have none of that and said "no mas."

Benny Leonard

From the beginning few had doubted that Benny Leonard would embrace a life in the square ring. He ducked regulations to be able to launch his professional boxing career at 15, got knocked out in his first fight, but came back to become one of the greatest lightweights in boxing history.

On one occasion he fought two guys (Sammy Marino and Smiling Kemp) in one day (December 25, 1911, the year he turned pro). He won both bouts, one by decision and the other by knock out. He was back in the ring 5 days later, knocking out Paddy Parker in 4 rounds. Early in the year that followed (January 18, 1912), he KOed Lewis Gibbs in 2 rounds and, on the next day, also KOed Willie Singer in 1 round.

But like Henry Armstrong who would follow in his footsteps 3 decades later, Leonard struggled in the early years of his professional career. After 54 fights, he barely managed to win 28 of them, losing 11, and the rest were either draws or no contests.

After 58 more fights he challenged Freddie Welsh for the latter's lightweight title on May 28, 1917 at the Manhattan S.C., New York, USA. It was a successful attempt (coming by way of TKO in the 9th) and so started his 6-year reign as lightweight king.

In 1922, he made an attempt to wrest the welterweight crown as well. But for a mental lapse on his part, he nearly succeeded.

In the title bout with Jack Britton, the welterweight champion, Leonard looked headed to a rousing win. He floored and hurt the champion in the 13th round, who was about to be counted out by the referee when Leonard hit him some more.

The referee disqualified Leonard and gave the fight to the defending champion.

Leonard was lording it over his opponents at about the same time when Jess Willard was heavyweight champion. At 6'6", Willard was so big a boxer in his era that he literally towered over his opponents. The problem with him was he looked awkward and moved even more awkwardly.

Thus Leonard provided contrast to the heavyweight champion. His skills level was obviously notches higher. Hence it was in this context that the press minted the term "pound for pound" champion, and people used it to refer to Leonard.

He was a picture of graceful aggression and cunning inside the ring. Often talking to his opponents, he was a master of tactically-defensive fighting as he was an explosive puncher.

Leonard's no-fear approach to combat was legendary. Sportswriters at the time noted how often he would come out of fights with the same unruffled and tidily combed hair he had when he first entered the ring. It implied, at least figuratively, that no fighter and no situation inside the ring frightened him.

He wowed the crowds with his boxing style; and the fans loved the way he bludgeoned his adver-

PROFILE SUMMARY			
Name:	Jack Dempsey	Professional Career Highlights	
Alias:	Manassa Mauler	Total Fights	83
Birth Name:	William Harrison Dempsey	Wins	66
Birth Place:	Manassa, Colorado, USA	Winning Percentage	79.52
Birth Date:	24 June 1895	Losses	6
Death Date:	31 May 1983	Draws	11
Nationality:	United States	NCs/Disqualifications	0
Residence:	Salt Lake City, Utah, USA	KOs	51
Stance:	Orthodox	KO Percentage	77.27
Height:	6'1" / 185 cm	Percentage of Quality Wins	71.43
Reach:	77" / 196 cm	Years Active	12

World Titles in Different Weight Divisions					
DIVISION	TOTAL DIV TITLES	FROM		TO	
		Month	Year	Month	Year
Heavyweight	1	July	1919	July	1926
TOTAL	1				

Right photo shows **Jack Dempsey** knocked outside of the ring by **Luis Angel Firpo**. Dempsey floored Firpo 7 times in the first round alone, but Firpo returned the favor, knocking Dempsey down once each in rounds 1 and 2. Dempsey climbed back into the ring and knocked Firpo out in that same fateful second round. **Photos by Google Images.**

saries into submission. A 1923 fight at the Yankee Stadium in New York against Lew Tendler attracted close to 60,000 paying fans—a record at the time.

He retired in 1925. But the 1929 stock market crash in the US, which buried away most of his earnings, forced him back to the ring to earn a living. He remained active until 1932. A TKO loss to Jimmy McLarnin in that year prompted him to hang up his gloves for good.

In retirement, he continued to be involved in boxing one way or the other. Ironically for one who showed no fear inside the ring, he died of heart attack while refereeing a boxing match.

Jack Johnson

One can say that Jack Johnson had the tough luck of having been a professional athlete at a place where, and in a time when, businessmen involved in boxing shied away from "colored" fighters for fear that paying fans may reject them.

And yet one can also say that Johnson was lucky for being a beneficiary of a prank dare. After he had beaten all contenders of consequence in the heavyweight division, Johnson put himself in a position to challenge Tommy Burns, then the heavyweight champion. But the latter avoided him by demanding a guaranteed purse of US$ 30,000. At the time the amount was outlandish, and was the equivalent of ensuring that a fight

PROFILE SUMMARY

Name:	Sam Langford	Professional Career Highlights	
Alias:	Boston Tar Baby	Total Fights	315
Birth Name:	Sam Langford	Wins	203
Birth Place:	Weymouth, Nova Scotia, Canada	Winning Percentage	64.44
Birth Date:	4 April 1883	Losses	47
Death Date:	12 January 1956	Draws	50
Nationality:	Canada	NCs/Disqualifications	15
Residence:	Boston, Massachusetts, USA	KOs	128
Stance:	Orthodox	KO Percentage	63.05
Height:	5'6½" / 169 cm	Percentage of Quality Wins	56.50
Reach:	72" / 183 cm	Years Active	25

World Titles in Different Weight Divisions

DIVISION	TOTAL DIV TITLES	FROM Month	Year	TO Month	Year
	0				
TOTAL	0				

Sam Langford recorded one of the most number of career fights in boxing history: 315. It was not uncommon for him to fight twice in a single day. Right photo shows **Langford** battling **Sam McVea** (whom he had fought inside the ring at least 15 times) in 1916. **Photos by Google Images.**

PROFILE SUMMARY			
Name:	Billy Conn	Professional Career Highlights	
Alias:	Pittsburgh Kid	Total Fights	77
Birth Name:	William David Conn	Wins	64
Birth Place:	East Liberty, PA, USA	Winning Percentage	83.12
Birth Date:	8 October 1917	Losses	12
Death Date:	29 May 1993	Draws	1
Nationality:	United States	NCs/Disqualifications	0
Residence:	Pittsburgh, PA, USA	KOs	15
Stance:	Orthodox	KO Percentage	23.44
Height:	6'1½" / 187 cm	Percentage of Quality Wins	84.78
Reach:	72" / 184 cm	Years Active	11

World Titles in Different Weight Divisions					
DIVISION	TOTAL DIV TITLES	FROM		TO	
		Month	Year	Month	Year
Light Heavyweight	1	July	1939	June	1941
TOTAL	1				

It is almost ironic that **Billy Conn** is best remembered not for his wins (who ruled as light heavyweight champion from 1939 to 1941), but for a loss to then heavyweight champion **Joe Louis**. Right photo shows Conn battling Louis on even terms in their first ring duel in 1941, before being KO'ed in the 13th of a scheduled 15-round title match. **Photos by Google Images.**

with Johnson would not happen.

Johnson hounded Burns anywhere the latter went, until a boxing promoter in Australia risked the huge amount of money he needed to stage a Burns-Johnson title fight.

On December 26, 2008, Johnson became the first black American to become a boxing champion by defeating Tommy Burns.

He reigned for 7 years. That reign was not totally majestic, however. Johnson flaunted his rebellious bent. He defied social convention. He attacked the racial standards of his time and did what colored people were expected not to do, such as by hanging out with white women in public.

The boxing constituency vowed not to have another colored champion. Even a large part of the African-American community disowned Johnson. He has unnecessarily dragged its members into a tense social environment.

In time he would come in conflict with the law. He fled his homeland, became a fugitive, and forced to campaign overseas.

He eventually returned to America and lost to Jess Willard, a hulk of a white man, on April 5, 1915.

Jack Dempsey

For one who did not get paid for winning the heavyweight crown against Jess Willard, Jack Dempsey's story surprises boxing students for being one of few financial successes in their post-boxing life.

As already mentioned earlier in this book, Dempsey ascended to the apex of prize fighting without his prize. His manager has lost his purse on a bet Dempsey would win the fight right in the first round. Although Dempsey did floor Willard 7 times in the opening round, the fight went on until the third round, when Willard was thoroughly beaten and unable to continue.

Perhaps Dempsey was himself to blame for his misfortune. Prior to his bout against Willard, Dempsey had a string of 25 wins, 24 of which coming by way of knockout (18 in the first round). Fans felt a Dempsey fight was good for as long as it lasted. And few of his fights lasted long enough to cover the full route.

Although his personal life often got him tagged with a bad press, fans came in droves to watch his fights. They liked the way he fought relentlessly and aggressively inside the ring. His rematch with Gene Tunney on September 23, 1926 at Philadelphia, USA, attracted 120,557 fans—a long-standing record for live gate attendance.

Dempsey thus became one of the highest paid athletes in his time. In retirement, he put up several business ventures and succeeded in them as well.

PROFILE SUMMARY			
Name:	Harry Greb	**Professional Career Highlights**	
Alias:	Pittsburgh Windmill	Total Fights	299
Birth Name:	Edward Henry Greb	Wins	260
Birth Place:	Pittsburgh, Pennsylvania, USA	Winning Percentage	86.96
Birth Date:	6 June 1894	Losses	20
Death Date:	22 October 1926	Draws	18
Nationality:	United States	NCs/Disqualifications	1
Residence:	Pittsburgh, Pennsylvania, USA	KOs	48
Stance:	Orthodox	KO Percentage	18.46
Height:	5'8" / 173 cm	Percentage of Quality Wins	87.50
Reach:	71" / 180 cm	Years Active	15

World Titles in Different Weight Divisions					
DIVISION	TOTAL DIV TITLES	FROM		TO	
		Month	Year	Month	Year
Middleweight	1	Aug	1923	Feb	1926
TOTAL	1				

Greatness can be measured by the quality of one's opposition and the challenge the latter brings to the ring. If heavyweight champion **Jack Dempsey** had a conqueror in light heavyweight **Gene Tunney**, Tunney had a conqueror in middleweight **Harry Greb** (left photo). **Photos by Google Images.**

PROFILE SUMMARY

Name:	Sugar Ray Leonard	Professional Career Highlights	
Alias:	Sugar	Total Fights	40
Birth Name:	Ray Charles Leonard	Wins	36
Birth Place:	Wilmington, North Carolina, USA	Winning Percentage	90.00
Birth Date:	17 May 1956	Losses	3
Death Date:	NA	Draws	1
Nationality:	United States	NCs/Disqualifications	0
Residence:	Palmer Park, Maryland, USA	KOs	25
Stance:	Orthodox	KO Percentage	69.44
Height:	5'10" / 178 cm	Percentage of Quality Wins	89.47
Reach:	74" / 188 cm	Years Active	12

World Titles in Different Weight Divisions

DIVISION	TOTAL DIV TITLES	FROM		TO	
		Month	Year	Month	Year
Welterweight	1	Nov	1979	Nov	1982
Light Middleweight	1	June	1981	June	1981
Middleweight	1	Apr	1987	May	1987
Light Heavyweight	1	Nov	1988	Feb	1989
TOTAL	4				

Sugar Ray Leonard mixed it up with the all-time greats of his era—the eighties. The big names in this decade included **Roberto Duran, Thomas Hearns**, and **Marvelous Marvin Hagler** (left photo). **Photos by Google Images and SI.**

Sam Langford

Sam Langford did not win a single world title. But his exploits inside the ring has earned for him worldwide acclaim.

Langford competed for 25 years, from 1902 to 1926. It was a time when prize fighters earn purses solely from live gate proceeds. It was therefore important for boxers like Langford to fight in as many places as he could to maximize their earnings.

Quite not surprisingly, Langford recorded one of the most number of career fights in boxing history: 315. It was not uncommon for him to fight twice in a single day.

He won 203 of his fights, for a career win clip of 64 percent. Of those wins, 128 of them were knockouts. When fans asked him why he often finished off an opponent early in the fight, the press had often quoted Langford as saying: "I have to catch that eleven-thirty train, you know."

Aside from his outstanding ring record, Langford often gave away height and heft to his opponents. Although he stood only at 5'6½, he competed as a heavyweight (in those times, most fights were conducted at the limitless—heavyweight—division anyway).

Some boxing experts had recognized Langford as one of the greatest heavyweights of all time. Nova Scotia likewise also cited him as the best athlete of the 20th century.

Ring wizardry was not enough to lift himself up as contender for the world crown, much less elevate him to the status of world titlist, however. He never got around fighting officially for a world crown, despite beating its top contenders. Racism in his era had something to do with it.

Billy Conn

After a not-so-impressive start as a professional boxer in 1934 (7 losses in his first 15 fights), Billy Conn terrorized the opposition by winning all 28 of his fights (with one draw) in the next two years.

Another winning streak in 1938 all the way up to 1941 (a solitary loss in 22 fights) catapulted him to the elite company of world boxing greats. On July 13, 1939, at age 22, he won the Light Heavyweight championship from Melio Bettina.

Ironically, Conn is best remembered not for his wins, but for a loss to then heavyweight cham-

PROFILE SUMMARY

Name:	Pernell Whitaker	Professional Career Highlights	
Alias:	Sweat Pea	Total Fights	46
Birth Name:	Pernell Whitaker	Wins	40
Birth Place:	Norfolk, Virginia, USA	Winning Percentage	86.96
Birth Date:	2 January 1964	Losses	4
Death Date:	NA	Draws	1
Nationality:	United States	NCs/Disqualifications	1
Residence:	Raleigh, North Carolina, USA	KOs	17
Stance:	Southpaw	KO Percentage	42.50
Height:	5'6" / 168 cm	Percentage of Quality Wins	84.62
Reach:	69" / 15 cm	Years Active	16

World Titles in Different Weight Divisions

DIVISION	TOTAL DIV TITLES	FROM		TO	
		Month	Year	Month	Year
Lightweight	1	Feb	1989	Jan	1992
Light Welterweight	1	Jul	1992	Jan	1993
Welterweight	1	Jul	1992	Apr	1997
Light Middleweight	1	Mar	1995	Dec	1995
TOTAL	4				

Two all-time greats, **Oscar de la Hoya** and **Pernell Whitaker**, locked in a battle for the WBC Welterweight crown on April 12, 1997 (left). After a 41-1 win-loss streak, Pernell lost to Oscar. **Photos by Google and SI.**

PROFILE SUMMARY

Name:	Mike Tyson	Professional Career Highlights	
Alias:	Iron	Total Fights	58
Birth Name:	Michael Gerard Tyson	Wins	50
Birth Place:	Brooklyn, New York, USA	Winning Percentage	86.21
Birth Date:	30 June 1966	Losses	6
Death Date:	NA	Draws	0
Nationality:	United States	NCs/Disqualifications	2
Residence:	Catskill, New York, USA	KOs	44
Stance:	Orthodox	KO Percentage	88.00
Height:	5'10" / 178 cm	Percentage of Quality Wins	84.00
Reach:	71" / 180 cm	Years Active	15

World Titles in Different Weight Divisions

DIVISION	TOTAL DIV TITLES	FROM		TO	
		Month	Year	Month	Year
Heavyweight	1	Nov	1986	Feb	1990
WBC (1986-1990)					
WBA (1987-1990)					
IBF (1987-1990)					
WBC Heavyweight		Mar	1996	Jun	2002
TOTAL	1				

A Serving of His Own Menu. Of **Mike Tyson's** 50 career wins, 44 of them ended by KO or TKO (the highest KO rate in this book). He lost a total of 6 fights, 5 of them also by KO or TKO (1 by disqualification). **Photos by Google Images.**

pion Joe Louis. The latter had toppled all contenders in his division in almost singular manner—by knockout.

Thus when Conn challenged the heavier Louis for the latter's crown, the fans went to watch his execution. But Conn proved to be a fine boxer. His speed made the opponent's punching power insignificant. As the bout progressed the fans realized it was Louis, not him, who risked being executed.

Conn did go for the kill. In the 13th round, thinking Louis was ready to go down, he brawled. It was a mistake. Louis saw an opening to counter and knocked Conn out in that round.

Harry Greb

Like Sam Langford, Harry Greb fought in an era where making a living from boxing relied on what the fans paid at the gates. He thus had to be inside the ring as much as he could to get ahead financially in his career.

Greb was a true warrior. Again like Langford, there were times when Greb fought twice in a single day; other times he entered the ring with a bruised face or a black eye.

Once he fought in an exhibition bout (against Kid Lewis) that turned into a serious match. Reacting

PROFILE SUMMARY

Name:	Julio Cesar Chavez	Professional Career Highlights	
Alias:	JC	Total Fights	115
Birth Name:	Julio Cesar Chavez Gonzalez	Wins	107
Birth Place:	Ciudad Obregon, Son, Mexico	Winning Percentage	93.04
Birth Date:	12 July 1962	Losses	6
Death Date:	NA	Draws	2
Nationality:	Mexico	NCs/Disqualifications	0
Residence:	Culiacan, Sinaloa, Mexico	KOs	86
Stance:	Orthodox	KO Percentage	80.37
Height:	5'7½" / 171 cm	Percentage of Quality Wins	78.38
Reach:	68" / 173 cm	Years Active	25

World Titles in Different Weight Divisions

DIVISION	TOTAL DIV TITLES	FROM		TO	
		Month	Year	Month	Year
WBC Super Featherweight	1	Sep	1984	Nov	1987
Lightweight WBA (1987-1989) WBC (1988-1989)	1	Nov	1987	Jan	1989
WBC Light Welterweight IBF (1990-1991)	1	May	1989/1994	Jan/Jun	1994/1996
TOTAL	3				

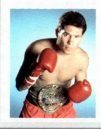 

Right photo shows **Julio Cesar Chavez Sr** versus **Pernell Whitaker,** just one his more than a hundred memorable fights. Chavez also matched his boxing skills with the likes of Oscar de la Hoya and Kostya Tszyu. **Photos by Google Images.**

to a vicious attack from his foe, Greb knocked Lewis out with a powerful left hook to the body.

His greatness can be viewed in the context of one's competition. If heavyweight champion Jack Dempsey had a conqueror in light heavyweight Gene Tunney, Tunney had a conqueror in middleweight Greb.

Greb competed in at least 299 fights throughout his career, winning 260 of them. He could have competed some more, but failing health kept him away from the ring. He was seriously injured in a car accident on August 21, 1925. He died a year later from complications brought about by eye surgery. He was 32.

Sugar Ray Leonard

There were 5 key reasons why boxing reached unprecedented levels of popularity in the 1980s. Sugar Ray Leonard was one of them. The other 4 would include Duran, Thomas Hearns, Marvin Hagler and satellite TV. Together, they created masterpieces out of boxing. But in individual match-ups among the top 4, Leonard has emerged as the best fighter. He has defeated all three, although the one against Hagler—a split decision—was controversial.

Leonard's rise to the top of professional boxing in his time was preceded by an outstanding amateur record. He was champion in almost all amateur boxing tournaments he participated in, highlighted by his winning the light welterweight gold medal in the 1976 Montreal (Canada) Olympics. As a professional, he was one of few fighters who won titles in at least 4 weight divisions—welterweight, light middleweight, middleweight and light heavyweight.

Pernell Whitaker

Like Sugar Ray Leonard and many other legendary professional boxers, Pernell Whitaker had an outstanding amateur stint. He won the lightweight gold medal during the 1984 Los Angeles Olympics.

He turned pro right after the Olympics. He was equally impressive as a professional fighter. Except for a single loss and a draw, he won all his first 42 bouts. He has beaten the top contenders in all the weight divisions where he competed. From 1989 to 1997, he has ruled at one time or

PROFILE SUMMARY					
Name:	Roy Jones Jr	Professional Career Highlights			
Alias:	Junior	Total Fights			59
Birth Name:	Roy Levesta Jones	Wins			54
Birth Place:	Pensacola, Florida, US	Winning Percentage			91.53
Birth Date:	16 January 1969	Losses			5
Death Date:	NA	Draws			0
Nationality:	United States	NCs/Disqualifications			0
Residence:	Pensacola, Florida, US	KOs			40
Stance:	Orthodox	KO Percentage			74.07
Height:	5'11" / 180 cm	Percentage of Quality Wins			90.38
Reach:	74" / 188 cm	Years Active			21
World Titles in Different Weight Divisions					
DIVISION	TOTAL DIV TITLES	FROM		TO	
		Month	Year	Month	Year
IBF Middleweight	1	May	1993	Nov	1994
IBF Super Middleweight	1	Nov	1994	Nov	1996
Light Heavyweight (WBC, WBA, IBF)	1	Aug	1997	May	2004
WBA Heavyweight	1	Mar	2003	Feb	2004
TOTAL	4				

In his prime, **Roy Jones Jr** was a masterpiece in motion inside the ring, such as the one shown at right, against **Eric Lucas** in 1996. He broke **Bob Fitzsimmon's** century-old record of winning belts from middleweight to heavyweight. **Photos by Google Images.**

another the lightweight, light welterweight, welterweight and light middleweight divisions.

Oscar De La Hoya halted his run on April 12, 1997 in his 10th defense of the welterweight title. Already 34 at this time, he dropped 3 more matches after that before finally retiring.

Mike Tyson

Like the young Duran, young Tyson was a frequent guest of the local police. And the New York police, too, would lend a hand in introducing Tyson to boxing. It was like monkey throwing turtle to the water. Everything suited to him fine. He searched anywhere for outlet of the psycho-social baggage that piled up from his troubled adolescent years. He found one in beck-busting.

The parallelism with Duran does not end there. Both of them went to war with the intent of courting bedlam, as if devastation was something to relish. They were ferocious, aggressive and explosive inside the ring. Like Jack Dempsey, Joe Louis and George Foreman before them, they evoked fear in the hearts of their foes—and for good reason. For these guys, knocking people out seemed like "all in a day's work."

Tyson started to compete in amateur boxing at 15. Even at this early stage, he already showed some habit of knocking people out. He held the record of the fastest knock out win, ever: 8 seconds. At 18, he won the national Golden Gloves championship—heavyweight division.

He turned pro at 19 and rocked the world of boxing right away. Thirty-eight wins in succession, all but 4 of them inside the distance. These four survivors, obviously, had the common sense of using their feet to run instead of their hands to fight.

On November 22, 1986, he became the youngest heavyweight champion in boxing history. He wrested the title from Trevor Berbick, who couldn't take much more punishment from Tyson after 2 rounds.

His knock out record of 44 out of 50 wins ranks at the top of the all-time list. It seemed the mere shadow of his glare could already stun his prey. Those who watched on TV his fight against Peter McNeely in 1995, for example, would recall the pre-fight ritual in the middle of ring where the referee mumbled the rules and asked the fighters to acknowledge each other with a glove shake. For several second that could have extended to a minute Tyson did not move a muscle, except one or two at the back his eyes—which followed McNeely as McNeely tensely shifted his body weight from left to right. McNeely grinned for what the viewers felt was cover for fear. When the bell rang, he charged at Tyson and got himself tagged instead. He lost in round 1.

There is another side of Tyson's story, however. Quite arguably still captive of his past, he easily got himself into trouble with the law. That kept him out of boxing at several points of his career, the longest period being the one in which he served time from 1992 to 1994 for rape conviction.

It was not good for his boxing career. After defending his title 11 times in more than 3 years before losing it to Buster Douglas in 1990, he did manage to recapture it from Frank Bruno 6 years later.

But people knew that his time as a prizefighter was up. Seven of his last 12 fights ended either in defeat or no contest. After Douglas, four more fighters (Evander Holyfield, Lennox Lewis, Danny Williams and Kevin McBride) beat him the way he beat the rest—by KO.

Julio Cesar Chavez Sr

Probably the greatest fighter that Mexico has ever produced, Julio Cesar Chavez is also one of the world's best boxers.

He was undefeated in his first 90 professional fights. Perhaps an even more awesome part of this extra-ordinary feat was that most of these wins (79 to be exact) did not go the distance. In the current list of greatest fighters, Chavez ranks third in terms of highest knock out rate. Only Mike Tyson (first) and Shane Mosley (second) had outperformed him in this category.

In that remarkable stretch he would eventually collect world titles in 3 different weight divisions—super featherweight, lightweight and light welterweight. He held these titles for a combined period of more than 11 years. Most notable among the opponents who bowed to him included Rocky Lockridge, Edwin Rosario, Jose Luis Ramirez (who had a 101-6-0 win-loss-draw record when they met), Roger Mayweather (twice, both TKO wins for Chavez), Alberto Cortes (undefeated in 44 fights), Angel Hernandez (undefeated in 37 fights), Frankie Mitchell (29-1-0), Hector Camacho (only one defeat in 42 fights), Marty Jakubowski (undefeated in

PROFILE SUMMARY					
Name:	Oscar De La Hoya	Professional Career Highlights			
Alias:	Golden Boy	Total Fights			45
Birth Name:	Oscar De La Hoya	Wins			39
Birth Place:	Montebello, CA, USA	Winning Percentage			86.67
Birth Date:	4 February 1973	Losses			6
Death Date:	NA	Draws			0
Nationality:	United States	NCs/Disqualifications			0
Residence:	Los Angeles, California, US	KOs			30
Stance:	Orthodox	KO Percentage			76.92
Height:	5'10½" / 179 cm	Percentage of Quality Wins			86.36
Reach:	73" / 185 cm	Years Active			16
World Titles in Different Weight Divisions					
DIVISION	TOTAL DIV TITLES	FROM		TO	
		Month	Year	Month	Year
Super Featherweight	1	Mar	1994	Jul	1994
Lightweight	1	Jul	1994	Jan	1996
Light Welterweight	1	Jun	1996	Apr	1997
Welterweight	1	Apr	1997	Jun	2000
Light Middleweight	1	June/May	2001/2006	Sep/May	2003/2007
Middleweight	1	Jun	2004	Sep	2004
TOTAL	6				

Oscar De La Hoya, Boxing's Golden Boy, has been considered as the biggest draw of the sport. Aside from boxing, he has also succeeded as businessman. **Photos by Google Images.**

37 fights), and Andy Holligan (no loss in 21 fights).

One of the most dramatic and unforgettable fights in boxing history pitted Chavez against Meldrick Taylor on March 17, 1990. It was a slam-bang contest. Chavez, in his signature non-stop, action-packed attacking style, tried to engage Taylor in a close-range fighting all throughout. But the unexpectedly game and unintimidated Taylor chose to box him, unloading shots with precision even as he was busy taking cover. He was leading Chavez on the judges' scorecards going to the final seconds of the fight. Most boxing fans who saw it conceded that Chavez was on his way to being beaten for the first time. But the Mexican showed his fighting heart to the end, until a fierce exchange of gloves in the closing seconds (something which Taylor could have avoided and run away with the win) hurt Taylor badly that the referee had to stop the fight and declare Chavez the winner by TKO.

His first loss came at his 92nd fight, a split decision setback to Frankie Randall on January 24, 1994. He quickly avenged that loss, however, when he upended Randall in 8 rounds in a rematch 4 months later.

His longest reign was at light welterweight, from 1989 to 1996. Earlier, he was super featherweight champion from 1984 to 1987; and

PROFILE SUMMARY

Name:	Shane Mosley	**Professional Career Highlights**	
Alias:	Sugar	Total Fights	54
Birth Name:	Shane Donte Mosley	Wins	46
Birth Place:	Lynwood, California, US	Winning Percentage	81.91
Birth Date:	7 September 1971	Losses	6
Death Date:	NA	Draws	0
Nationality:	United States	NCs/Disqualifications	1
Residence:	Pomona, California, US	KOs	39
Stance:	Orthodox	KO Percentage	84.78
Height:	5'9" / 175 cm	Percentage of Quality Wins	85.37
Reach:	74" / 188 cm	Years Active	18

World Titles in Different Weight Divisions

DIVISION	TOTAL DIV TITLES	FROM		TO	
		Month	Year	Month	Year
IBF Lightweight	1	Aug	1997	Apr	1999
WBC Welterweight	1	Aug	2000	Jan	2002
WBA Welterweight		Jan	2009	Jan	2010
WBC/WBA Light Middleweight	1	Sep	2003	Mar	2004
TOTAL	**3**				

When history writes about **Shane Mosley**, his being second to **Mike Tyson** in terms of having the highest knock out rate in boxing (at least in this list) is sure to be highlighted. **Photos by Google Images.**

lightweight champion from 1987 to 1989.

Chavez started to uncharacteristically suffer losses in 1996, and onwards until 2005, when he retired at age 43. Devastating losses to Oscar De La Hoya (twice, by TKO), Kostya Tszyu and Grover Wiley forced his otherwise reluctant slide to retirement.

Chavez had a career record of 107 wins, 6 losses and 2 draws out of 115 total fights, for an exceptional 93 percent winning percentage. Of the 5 opponents who defeated him, all were beaten in rematches (except De La Hoya; and there was no rematch against Kostya Tszyu). One can argue today that Chavez in effect lost only twice in 115 ring battles, and get away with it unchallenged.

Roy Jones Jr

The guy made himself one-of-a-kind when he jumped from middleweight all the way up to heavyweight, collecting titles at every stop. No other fighter, living or dead, has done that since 1897, when England's Bob Fitzsimmons crossed the imaginary boxing divide. At that time, there was only one world boxing champion (always a heavyweight, ie, until Fitzsimmons came along), and there were only two weight divisions (the heavyweight and the "lighter weight," which comprised all other weights under heavyweight). Fitzsimmons was in the lighter weight division when he defeated the then current world champion to become the new world boxing champion.

Jones weighed 193 pounds (up from 175 pounds in his previous bout 6 months earlier), when he snatched part of the heavyweight diadem from John Ruiz on March 1, 2003. He gave away 33 pounds to Ruiz, who weighed 226 pounds. But the disparity in weight hardly showed as Jones cruised to a 12-round unanimous decision win over Ruiz.

Jones was proud of his work. He said during the post-fight interview: "I know what people are going to say, but there is nothing wrong with John Ruiz. Like a lot of other guys I fought, he was just slower than me. And I kind of out thought him."

Indeed, most guys he fought looked like PODs (persons with disabilities, no disrespect intended to them) in comparison to him. The phenomenal Jones earned the "Fighter of the Decade" award from the Boxing Writers Association of America for his sterling ring performance in the late 80s until the early 2000s. A quick look at what he accomplished, so far: a solitary loss (which should have been a win, in the first place) in 50 fights, all but 9 of them coming by way of either knock out or technical knock out.

That loss came on March 21, 1997 in a light heavyweight title bout against Montell Griffin. Jones knocked Griffin down in the 7th round of that fight. In the 9th, Jones had Griffin in even more dire situation. A wicked right—sleek as an arrow and precise as a computer-aided missile—put Griffin down on one knee, ready to roll over like an uprooted gmelina. But Jones could not hold back his excitement; he hit Griffin two more times. It was a clear and obvious foul. Referee Tony Perez had no other option but to disqualify him and gave the fight to Griffin. Jones led on the scorecards of two judges—77-75 (Chuck Hasset) and 76-75 (Terry Smith)—when the fight was stopped.

Jones quickly removed that blight on his resume, however. He avenged that loss to Griffin in a rematch 5 months later, on August 17, 1997, with three—possibly 5—exclamation marks. He knocked the guy out in the first round.

Jones was no stranger to strange fight outcomes. He was one of the boxers sent by the US to the 1988 Seoul Olympics after topping the Olympic trials for the light middleweight division. After getting through the qualifying rounds, he met local bet Park Si-Hun in the finals for the light middleweight gold. He dominated Park all throughout their bout, but ended up losing by a 2-3 decision.

One judge later admitted that in his view Jones clearly won. He voted for Park, nonetheless, because he was sure his fellow judges would vote for Jones, and he didn't want the host country's boxer to be embarrassed by losing a 5-0 decision. Interestingly, organizers awarded him the Val Barker Trophy, which is reserved for boxers whose performance in the Games had been found above the norm.

At the pro ranks, his superiority over the competition has been as telling. He has ruled 4 divisions—middleweight, super middleweight, light heavyweight and heavyweight—one at a time, in his 21 (still active) years as boxer.

Jones is a man of many talents. Aside from boxing, he dabbles as a businessman, a basketball player, a recording artist, a music manager, an actor, etc.

PROFILE SUMMARY

Name:	Bernard Hopkins	Professional Career Highlights	
Alias:	The Executioner	Total Fights	58
Birth Name:	Bernard Hopkins	Wins	51
Birth Place:	Philadelphia, Pennsylvania, US	Winning Percentage	87.93
Birth Date:	15 January 1965	Losses	5
Death Date:	NA	Draws	1
Nationality:	United States	NCs/Disqualifications	1
Residence:	Philadelphia, Pennsylvania, US	KOs	32
Stance:	Orthodox	KO Percentage	62.75
Height:	6'1" / 185 cm	Percentage of Quality Wins	82.50
Reach:	75" / 191 cm	Years Active	20

World Titles in Different Weight Divisions

DIVISION	TOTAL DIV TITLES	FROM		TO	
		Month	Year	Month	Year
Middleweight	1	Apr	1995	Jul	2005
IBF (1995-2005) WBC (2001-2005) WBA (2001-2005) WBO (2004-2005)					
Light Heavyweight	1	Jun	2006	Apr	2008
TOTAL	2				

Bernard Hopkins in two of his masterful wins against marquee opponents: vs **Kelly Pavlik** (left) and vs **Oscar De La Hoya** (right). Photos by Google Images.

Oscar De La Hoya

For the first time in history since boxing became part of the Olympics, the US was almost shut out of the gold hunt in that event at the Barcelona Games in 1992. Thanks to Oscar De La Hoya, the US Boxing Team did not go home totally empty-handed. De La Hoya won the gold in the featherweight division and, from then on, the world would refer to him as the "Golden Boy."

After capping his tour in amateur boxing with a flourish, he turned professional late in that same year and fought twice. He became busier in the next 7 years, fighting at least 4 times each year. Throughout this period, his reputation as a world-class boxer has been validated many times over. His record was impeccable—no loss in 31 fights, 25 of them by knock out or TKO. He was not only winning big; he was also winning against big names. By this time, he had already beaten at least 19 world champions or top-ranked contenders, collecting world titles in 4 weight divisions along the way.

But the best for De La Hoya was yet to come. He spent the next 9 years of his professional boxing career seeking out top-level competition. In this period he faced 14 world champions, with at least 6 of them future Hall-of- Famers, and in the process collecting 2 more world titles in yet different weight divisions.

Although not as successful as in the first half of his career, his following has multiplied the world over. Endowed with looks and physique that made boxing fans out of movie fans, he attracted hordes of spectators into his fights like nobody before him ever did. People mobbed him. They adored him. Wherever he fought, boxing venues burst to the brim—and for the first time the boxing public had now constituted more and more shrieking female fans. On the May 5, 2007 fight with Floyd Mayweather, 2.15 million homes in America—a record—paid an average of US$ 56 to watch it via HBO's pay-per-view feed. There simply was no stopping the fans' attraction to the glitter of the Golden Boy. No doubt about it, Oscar was boxing's mega star.

De La Hoya got credit for being a performer. He had talent and skills that won fights for him. He has defeated the likes of Pernell Whitaker, Julio Cesar Chavez, Hector Camacho, among others—all at the top of most greatest-fighters-of-all-time lists. His competitive instinct denied chances for the unfit to survive.

What separated De La Hoya from the other all-time greats of boxing was the quality of fighters he fought. The career win average of his opponents was 88 %, which was even higher than his own career win percentage at 86. For one who collected world championships in 6 different weight divisions, this meant not only testing his own limits, it also meant testing the limits of the best fighters out there.

At some point he started to touch base with the business side of boxing, projecting the image of one who thinks and manages things rather than one who thinks and brawls. In 2001, he put up Golden Boy Promotions (as part of Golden Boy Enterprises) to stage his own fights. In 2007, he bought The Ring Magazine, among other media outfits, and put up several businesses and not-for-profit organizations.

In time, his management skills, too, would be evident and in harness. His businesses, led by the Golden Boy Promotions, grew. Marquee names in boxing—Shane Mosley, Bernard Hopkins, Marco Antonio Barrera, Ricky Hatton—became part of his promotional outfit one way or the other. For years it seemed there was no major boxing event that did not have Golden Boy Promotions as one of its organizers. De La Hoya made tons of money both inside and outside the ring. For many, he was like a trailblazer, succeeding financially in a sport where most of the legends before him had gone bankrupt as soon as they retired.

Shane Mosley

In a fair contest, beating a great boxer means you are a greater boxer. Sugar Shane Mosley has twice beaten a great competitor in Oscar De La Hoya, and that should be enough to ensure his lofty standing in places where the likes of De La Hoya are revered.

Indeed the Ring Magazine has recognized him as pound for pound champion in 2000 and 2001 during which time he outclassed, aside from De La Hoya, Antonio Diaz, Shannon Taylor and Adrian Stone.

And yet Mosley had a lot more to show. Like most fighters in the all-time greats list, he showed his class early. He could box and he could punch. He thrived in striking from long distance as much as in toe-to-toe middle-of-the-ring action. He packed power in both hands. In the current list, only Mike Tyson has a higher KO rate—88 percent to Mike, 85 percent

PROFILE SUMMARY			
Name:	Floyd Mayweather Jr	Professional Career Highlights	
Alias:	Money / Pretty Boy	Total Fights	41
Birth Name:	Floyd Joy Mayweather Jr	Wins	41
Birth Place:	Grand Rapids, Michigan, US	Winning Percentage	100.00
Birth Date:	24 February 1977	Losses	0
Death Date:	NA	Draws	0
Nationality:	United States	NCs/Disqualifications	0
Residence:	Nevada, United States	KOs	25
Stance:	Orthodox	KO Percentage	60.98
Height:	5'8" / 173 cm	Percentage of Quality Wins	100.00
Reach:	72" / 183 cm	Years Active	13

World Titles in Different Weight Divisions					
DIVISION	TOTAL DIV TITLES	FROM		TO	
		Month	Year	Month	Year
WBC Super Featherweight	1	Oct	1998	Apr	2002
WBC Lightweight	1	Apr	2002	Jan	2004
WBC Light Welterweight	1	Jun	2005	Dec	2005
Welterweight (IBF, WBC)	1	Apr	2006	Jun	2008
WBC Light Middleweight	1	May	2007	Jul	2007
TOTAL	5				

PREY NUMBER 39. Master of defense and all-around technique, top ring predator **Floyd Mayweather Jr** has beaten all 40 ring opponents (in 41 fights) he has faced so far. He decisioned **Juan Manual Marquez** (right) for his 39th win. **Photos by Google Images.**

for Mosley. No wonder his resume stood out. He went 39 and 0 before losing to the late Vernon Forrest, his tormentor way back in their amateur days.

At the time of his first defeat to Forrest (Mosley lost again to Forrest in a rematch), he was already on the 9th year of his boxing career, and relatively old at 31. Either he started to show signs of wear and tear or the competition for him has become tougher to overcome, but Mosley seemed to have ceased being Mosley since then. His winning average declined, winning "only" 8 in the next 14 grueling ring battles.

Overall, however, his achievements remained a cut above the ordinary. Some attributes of Mosley's success merit a little mention. For one, he has shown lots of courage in bucking the odds. It might be fair, even, to say that he had a knack for winning fights many people thought he had little chances of winning.

Although undefeated after 24 fights, he was an underdog when he challenged Philip Holiday, also undefeated after 31 fights, for the lightweight title on August 2, 1997. He was also underdog when he clobbered De La Hoya for the first time. And then, given the previous few fights he came from, he was not given much chance against Antonio Margarito to reclaim his welterweight championship. In all cases, he proved the doubters wrong.

For another, Mosley has yet to lose in a very lopsided fashion, much less an abbreviated one. His losses could be considered competitive up to the final second of each bout. A few more flurry of punches from him could have swung the decision in his favor, and avoided one or two blemishes in his record. Moreover, while he has already lost 5 times, only 3 fighters have actually beaten him (two—Forrest and Ronald Wright—have defeated him twice).

With what he has accomplished—world titles in 3 different divisions—he has little else to prove inside the ring. But at 38, Mosley still competes at a high level, something which other great fighters could only hope to do.

Bernard Hopkins

The longest-reigning middleweight champion in history did not look like one when he climbed the professional ring the first time. His opponent, Clinton Mitchell, trashed him by majority decision in a 4 rounder. Signs showed the squared ring was not meant for him, so he shied away from it in the next 18 months. But like a criminal who keeps coming back to the scene of the crime, the man who branded himself as "The Executioner" gave himself another shot at prizefighting.

Returning and claiming his first win in the early part of 1990 at age 25, Bernard Hopkins was, by the sport's common measure, a late bloomer. But when he did bloom, he let everyone notice.

He sprinted to 22 straight wins in 3 years after his first failed attempt. After 2 years and 4 more fights since Roy Jones Jr halted him at fight number 24 in 1993, he challenged Segundo Mercado, at age 29, for the latter's middleweight crown.

The result was a draw. It was not enough for him to wrest the championship, although it seemed sufficient to label him as a spent force at that stage of his career.

But he kept coming back, and in a rematch with Mercado 4 months later, he made sure he ran away with the title by halting the defending champion in 7 rounds. Hopkins, by then, was 30 years old.

While some fighters hang up their gloves at that age, Hopkins went on to rule the division for the next 11 years. He defended his title 20 times, until Jermain Taylor spoiled his record-breaking reign in 2005. One may notice that the way he defended his title indicated an achievement that was far from ordinary. Fifteen of his 18 challengers had a career win percentage of 90 percent or higher at the time they contended for Hopkins' title. Two of the 15—Glen Johnson and Felix Trinidad, both future Hall of Fame candidates—had perfect winning records. All of this signified one thing: Hopkins tested his ability against the best there were in the division, and he passed the test.

At 41, Hopkins looked farther ahead. On June 6, 2006, he captured the Light Heavyweight championship after defeating Antonio Tarver via unanimous decision in 12 rounds. His reign as light heavyweight titlist ended in less than 2 years, however. After defending it against Ro-

PROFILE SUMMARY

Name:	Manny Pacquiao	Professional Career Highlights	
Alias:	Pacman / The Greatest	Total Fights	56
Birth Name:	Emmanuel Dapidran Pacquiao	Wins	51
Birth Place:	Kibawe, Bukidnon, Philippines	Winning Percentage	91.07
Birth Date:	17 December 1978	Losses	3
Death Date:	NA	Draws	2
Nationality:	Philippines	NCs/Disqualifications	0
Residence:	Gen Santos City, Philippines	KOs	38
Stance:	Southpaw	KO Percentage	75.51
Height:	5'6½" / 169 cm	Percentage of Quality Wins	92.11
Reach:	67" / 170 cm	Years Active	15

World Titles in Different Weight Divisions

DIVISION	TOTAL DIV TITLES	FROM Month	FROM Year	TO Month	TO Year
WBC Flyweight	1	Dec	1998	Sep	1999
IBF Super Bantamweight	1	Jun	2001	Oct	2003
Featherweight (Ring)	1	Nov	2003	Mar	2005
WBC Super Featherweight	1	Mar	2008	Jun	2008
WBC Lightweight	1	Jun	2008	Feb	2009
IBO Light Welterweight	1	May	2009	Nov	2009
WBO Welterweight	1	Nov	2009	Mar	2010
TOTAL	6				

Non-believers question how **Manny Pacquiao** could jump from 130 lbs against **Juan Manual Marquez** in 2008 to 140 lbs against **Ricky Hatton** (right) and again farther up to 147 against Miguel Cotto, both in 2009. Fact is **Pacquiao** on fight night itself had consistently weighed from 144 lbs (against Morales in 2006) to 149 lbs (against Clottey in 2010).
Photos by Google Images.

nald Wright in 2007, he was out pointed by the undefeated Joe Calzaghe in 2008.

And just as it looked his slide towards retirement looked irreversible, Hopkins, at 43, gave the skeptics something to ponder about when he whipped Kelly Pavlik, undefeated in 34 top-level battles and Ring Magazine's light heavyweight ruler, in 12 rounds.

Hopkins continues to be a force to be reckoned with—and an attractive merchandise—if offers for him to step inside the ring one more time can be made as indication. The current buzz within the boxing community is for him to face Roy Jones Jr in a rematch 16 years after they did it the first time. What keeps it from happening soon, however, may have something to do with the price tag of either fighter.

Meantime, he too has diversified himself—along with Oscar De La Hoya and Shane Mosley—from boxing to business, as an executive of Golden Boy Promotions.

Floyd Mayweather Jr

The way Floyd Mayweather fights may not impress those who loved the way Jack Dempsey and Joe Louis fought. But Mayweather fights not to impress; he fights to win. And he delivers. It will be hard not to concede that he is master of the craft. To argue against Mayweather's boxing skills would be to argue against the facts: 40 wins in 40 professional career fights.

While the likes of Julio Cesar Chavez (undefeated in his first 91 fights), Willie Pep (undefeated in his first 62 fights) or Mike Tyson (undefeated going to his 42nd fight) could boast of better records, the stories behind Mayweather's rampage should provide an unassailable argument for what makes him special. At least 22 world champions, or at least would-be world champions—never mind the rest—have tried to outbox him. None of them succeeded.

Some analysts once pushed the notion that Mayweather's being a product of failure and experience has made him the exceptional fighter that he is today. He comes from a family of boxers. His father, Floyd Sr., has campaigned in the welterweight class. Floyd Sr's career, overall, could be rated as above average. But being active at a time when the likes of Thomas Hearns and Sugar Ray Leonard were at the peak of their careers almost meant the rest of the field had little chances of outshining any or both of them. In fact when Floyd Sr and Leonard eventually met, Floyd took a beating from Leonard with such savagery that it must have compelled Floyd Jr to imbibe, more than anything else, the value of defense. That, in a simplistic way of looking at it, should explain why Floyd Jr has probably surpassed the exploits of Benny Leonard and Willie Pep as the defensive geniuses of the game.

Jeff and Roger Mayweather are uncles, the latter being the most successful among the 3 elders. Roger rose to become a 2-time world champion. Nevertheless, he too, has experienced failure and punishment inside the ring, such as the one he got from Kostya Tszu.

Floyd Sr and Roger both graduated from ring action to become trainers. If the number of fighters they helped win championships was any indication, then there is no doubt that both of them have been successful as trainers as well, perhaps even more successful than being fighters. And Floyd Jr had the good fortune of being at the right place and time to benefit from the experience and know-how of Floyd Sr, Roger and Jeff.

Floyd's rise to superstardom status has boosted his value as entertainer. And he knows it. After he defeated Oscar De La Hoya in 2007, he retired instead of accepting offers of a rematch that did not satisfy his idea of fair compensation. At any rate he resurfaced to fight and eventually knock out Ricky Hatton towards the latter part of that year.

Floyd Jr had been at the top of most pound for pound rankings (the one published by the Ring Magazine being the most widely-accepted, if not the most credible, of them) since 2005. When he retired a second time after the Hatton fight, Manny Pacquiao took his place in the pound for pound rankings.

He resurfaced yet again in 2009 to fight Juan Manual Marquez, whom he beat by unanimous decision in 12 rounds. Some say his return was driven by a desire to reclaim his pound for pound title; others contend that Floyd Jr—who has made "Money" as an official nickname—is up to some schemes designed to cash in on his celebrity status. Others say he is motivated by both pride and money.

Manny Pacquiao

If Floyd Mayweather fights to win, Manny Pacquiao fights—in his own words—"to make the fans happy."

Pacquiao knows what he is talking about and people understand where he is coming from. When he was too young to make a decent living for himself and his family, life was so hard that controlling body weight was forced not by boxing rules but by lack of food to eat. "I understand," he said, "how it feels when people go hungry."

Every Philippine centavo was gold to the Pacquiao household. Which was why affluence became Manny Pacquiao when he earned his first paychecks of a hundred pesos (about 2 US dollars) fighting as a youngster in village-level fiestas. This is how relative reality is and that was how he valued hard-earned money. That was then. Today, he earns billions of Philippine pesos from boxing and commercial appearances, but his appreciation of each hard-earned peso remains the same.

He knows boxing fans spend equally good hard-earned money to watch his fights. He swears it's his job, as a professional fighter, to ensure they get their money's worth every time they see him perform.

When people watch Pacquiao fight, they see an incredible small-sized package of ferocity and aggression let loose inside the ring. What they may not see is what burns at the core of that package, the one that fuels such a huge amount of energy and passion—courage.

It takes courage to be able to continually honor one's commitment. It takes courage to make the fans happy and keep them from being disappointed.

>
>
> **Evander Holyfied**, 4-time world heavy weight champion, on **Manny Pacquiao:**
>
> *His humility is a great thing, and he fights. He does not complain, and he throws a lot of punches. He comes to fight and you know what you're going to get when you fight Manny Pacquiao... Manny takes on all comers and in his mind it is simple...you want to fight? Let's fight! Outside of the ring, he is humble.*
>
> As reported by **Brad Cooney**, Examiner.com on 16 October 2010

And courage—the heart of a warrior—is what makes Pacquiao the world's greatest fighter that he has become. Courage allowed him to challenge what lurked behind the unknown: whether it was, in search of his future in boxing, a strange life in the city where he knew no one and no one knew him; how a fight wish would play out against, for example, one of then boxing's hottest properties in Marco Antonio Barrera; coping with size disadvantage as in the case of fighting Oscar De La Hoya; the impossibility of moving up in weight and continuing to dominate the opposition; and try to see what it takes to test the limits of a world-class athlete, like himself.

Early in life Pacquiao knew he would become a boxing champion. The problem was, given the limited choices which his poor family had, he did not have ready resources to get there.

So he took odd jobs to keep body and soul together, as it were, while his dream of making it big in boxing someday continued to consume his waking hours. He left grade school to focus on making a living, and on living his dream.

But the hardships of life remained unforgiving to the Pacquiao household. They came in many forms, in addition to material want. The father, who left earlier to take a better-paying job, eventually left for good. The second of 6 siblings, Manny had to step up—in the traditional ways of a Filipino family set-up—and take the survival cudgels for the family. "Don't worry, Ma," the 14-year-old Manny vowed to his mother, "I will take care of this." He was referring to the financial and emotional problems of the family.

He soon left General Santos City, his hometown, for Manila, the big city, with nobody at home aware of it. He left a note, however, explaining his departure.

Several months later, Dionisia, Manny's mother, received by post a letter from Manny asking parental consent (in lieu of professional license) and excitedly telling her to watch him fight on national television. It was January in 1995 and, from then on, Dionisia and the entire Filipino nation found itself glued to television whenever Manny climbed the ring to fight.

It turned out Pacquiao was not only a performer; he was also a winner. From the time he turned professional at 16 to the present (he turned 31 on December 17, 2009), he has already won world titles in 7 different weight divisions. No other fighter in all of boxing history has reached that height of achievement.

By 2008, after beating the highly-favored De La Hoya, Pacquiao has blossomed to become a global celebrity. Acclaimed in 2009 by Times Magazine as one of the world's most influential persons, Pacquiao is also one of the world's richest athletes.

To Floyd Mayweather Jr's eternal envy, Pacquiao has also been awarded the title of "Fighter of the Decade" by the Boxing Writers Association of America.

Fifteen years after he left General Santos to find his star in the boxing universe, he has returned as a hero. He kept his promise and made his mother proud. In the succeeding pages, this book shall explain why Manny "The Pacman" Pacquiao is the greatest pound-for-pound boxer of all time.

To do that, the 22 all-time greats mentioned in the foregoing pages further undergo a rating process prescribed in this book. As we noted earlier, any attempt to rate the mentioned boxers can be very subjective. What this book intends to accomplish is add value to the process by using, to its practical limit, quantitative analysis.

The GOAT Debate

There are several (and quite obvious) things that make all-time greats lists or rankings open to question. One is the difficulty of capturing each athletic achievement in a single plane of quantitative analysis. If this was possible, then much of the subjective information that goes into the ratings process would be minimized.

Boxers Competed Under Different Conditions

It is hard to quantify the relative worth of boxers being rated for many reasons. One reason would be due to the different conditions and circumstances under which the fighters pursued their respective careers. Worldviews, for one, differed from one boxer to the other. If Sam Langford, for example, who was active from 1902 to 1926, were conscious of his being rated one day as an all-time great, would he have won more than half of the fights he lost? On the other hand, is Floyd Mayweather Jr conscious of his pound for pound standing? We may speculate that all Langford wanted was to make a living from prizefighting; thus to maximize his earnings, he fought once a week for the most part of his peak years. He did not prepare for his fights as rigid as, say, Mayweather would, who, undoubtedly, is fully conscious of how his ranking may sink or soar. And so Langford lost 47 (15 percent) of his 315 career fights, which puts him way off the standard set by Mayweather who has yet to lose in 40 fights. And yet Langford (standing at 5'6½") has started at 150 pounds or even less, and went on to win 64 percent of his fights in the heavyweight division. That would be the equivalent of Mayweather competing in the light heavyweight division. Would Mayweather win a single fight in the light heavyweight division, say against the likes of Roy Jones Jr? That would be one compelling consideration in evaluating the relative pound-for-pound value of fighters who competed in different eras and across weight divisions.

Related to worldviews (or perspectives) would be the existing commercial and cultural environment within which the fighters got to practice their craft. Again to cite Langford, who competed at a time when television and other technological gadgets that make the process of mass communication convenient were yet unheard of, making money from professional boxing was limited to what the fans paid at the gates of the boxing arena. (Elite boxers today get paid from various sources, such as TV royalties and pay-per-view sales, aside of course from guaranteed purses). To earn more money, one needed to hop from one arena to the other, either in the same city or the next, just like Langford did. (During his time, it was not rare for a fighter to fight twice in a single day!). Thus adequate physical training and preparation could not be remotely possible during those earlier times. They did not benefit from the same amount of rigor being applied by elite boxers today. This therefore makes it difficult to say that Langford could not be as great as Mayweather on the basis of their ring records.

In another context, one can say that the likes of Langford, a black man, were not fully tested because social norms prevented them from contending for world titles. Thus they hardly got around to compete against top-level opposition.

The Rules Evolved

The rules that governed boxing during the time of Benny Leonard and Jack Dempsey differed from the rules during the time of Muhammad Ali, Mike Tyson and Floyd Mayweather. What easily comes to mind when one talks about boxing rules are the weight divisions. The number of weight divisions has not only increased or decreased, the weight limits for a particular division has also kept changing over time. In earlier times, it was not unusual for a fighter to give away 10 pounds or more to this opponent. This seldom happens now, except in the heavyweight divisions. Thus winning fights in earlier times could be more significant than winning fights today, given such a weight handicap.

Another variable rule had something to do with fixing the number of rounds for a contest. In the early 20th century, fighters could agree to fight for as many as 45 rounds. If such a rule had similarly been applied to Mayweather, one could ask if he would have been able to stay unbeaten after 40 fights.

Also, during those times, it was not uncommon for contending parties to agree on either a "No Decision" or "Draw" if the fight went the distance. This explains why Sam Langford, for example, had 50 draws and 15 no contests from his total recorded fights of 315. Again if such a rule had similarly applied to Mayweather, one could speculate if he would have been able to keep the spotless record that he is wont to flaunt around. (As a footnote, we keep on citing the case of Mayweather as an example because he had been quoted in media more than once as saying things to the effect that his unblemished record is compelling basis for his having merited the pound for pound title. This book argues that such a contention is far from being unassailable.)

Quality and Depth Of Opposition

Another factor that makes comparison among fighters difficult would be the quality and depth of opposition against which, again, arguably differed among fighters in different eras and weight divisions. We can cite the case of Sugar Ray Robinson as an example. He won 173 out of his total 200 career fights (86.5 percent). But of all his opponents, only 12 of them had a career win percentage of at least 90 at the time of their encounter. That says something about the quality of opposition Robinson had. And of those 12 quality fights, he won only 7 times (58.3 percent). This suggests that when confronted with quality opposition, Robinson performed way below his standard.

A related indicator would be the depth of opposition. The density of active fighters differed across eras, with that of earlier times appearing to be less than what it is at present. An example would be Henry Armstrong, who fought many of his opponents several times—say against Perfecto Fernandez whom he faced 8 times inside the ring. Sam Langford fought Harry Mills 17 times, against Sam McVea 15 times, against Joe Jeannette 14 times, among others.

Criteria For Ranking

In view of the practical issues related to ranking the greatest boxers of all time, pound for pound, there is need for making sense out of available information in a less opinionated manner. To make the exercise somewhat more objective, this book applied the following criteria: The List, The Belt, and The Win. Each criterion will be explained below:

The List

The List defers to the analysis and opinion that went into three of boxing's most respected chroniclers—namely: The Ring Magazine, Associated Press, ESPN. But since these lists have been published years ago (eg The Ring came out with its list circa 1999, AP published its list in 2002), The List also makes use of Ring Magazine's Annual Pound-For-Pound list, which was published for the first time in 1989. This ensures that nobody is left out in the evaluation process. Furthermore, The List also adopts the results of a worldwide online poll in 2009.

THE LIST (50%)

NAME OF BOXERS	The Ring Magazine		Associated Press		ESPN		The Greatest Ever		The Ring Pound For Pound List (since 1989)		Ave Score	Points	SCORING SYSTEM	
	Rank	Score	Rank	Score	Rank	Score	Rank	Score	Rank	Score			RANK	SCORE
Sugar R Robinson	1	100.00	1	100.00	1	100.00	1	100.00	x	0.00	80.00	40.00	1	100.00
Henry Armstrong	2	95.45	3	86.67	3	86.67	x	0.00	x	0.00	67.20	33.60	2	95.45
Muhammad Ali	3	90.91	2	93.33	2	93.33	3	90.91	x	0.00	73.70	36.85	3	90.91
Joe Louis	4	86.36	4	80.00	4	80.00	x	0.00	x	0.00	61.59	30.80	4	86.36
Roberto Duran	5	81.82	7	60.00	6	66.67	x	0.00	x	0.00	52.12	26.06	5	81.82
Willie Pep	6	77.27	5	73.33	5	73.33	x	0.00	x	0.00	55.98	27.99	6	77.27
Benny Leonard	8	53.33	8	53.33	7	60.00	x	0.00	x	0.00	41.67	20.83	7	72.73
Jack Johnson	x	0.00	x	0.00	8	68.18	x	0.00	x	0.00	17.05	8.52	8	68.18
Jack Dempsey	x	0.00	6	77.27	9	63.64	x	0.00	x	0.00	35.23	17.61	9	63.64
Sam Langford	x	0.00	x	0.00	10	59.09	x	0.00	x	0.00	14.77	7.39	10	59.09
Billy Conn	x	0.00	9	63.64	x	0.00	x	0.00	x	0.00	15.91	7.96	11	54.55
Harry Greb	7	72.73	10	59.09	x	0.00	x	0.00	x	0.00	32.96	16.48	12	50.00
Sugar Ray Leonard	9	63.64	x	0.00	x	0.00	x	0.00	x	0.00	15.91	7.96	13	45.45
Pernell Whitaker	10	59.09	x	0.00	x	0.00	x	0.00	x	0.00	14.77	7.39	14	40.91
Mike Tyson	x	0.00	x	0.00	x	0.00	x	0.00	8	68.18	17.05	8.52	15	36.36
Julio Cesar Chavez	x	0.00	x	0.00	x	0.00	x	0.00	1--3	95.45	23.86	11.93	16	31.82
Roy Jones Jr	x	0.00	x	0.00	x	0.00	x	0.00	1--3	95.45	23.86	11.93	17	27.27
Oscar dela Hoya	x	0.00	x	0.00	x	0.00	x	0.00	4--7	79.55	19.89	9.94	18	22.73
Shane Mosley	x	0.00	x	0.00	x	0.00	x	0.00	4--7	79.55	19.89	9.94	19	18.18
Bernard Hopkins	x	0.00	x	0.00	x	0.00	x	0.00	4--7	79.55	19.89	9.94	20	13.64
Floyd Mayweather	x	0.00	x	0.00	x	0.00	x	0.00	1--3	95.45	23.86	11.93	21	9.09
Manny Pacquiao	x	0.00	x	0.00	x	0.00	2	94.45	4--7	79.55	35.00	17.50	22	4.55

The mentioned 3 lists have rankings of up to 100 all-time greats. This book, however, has limited itself in its evaluation to the top 10 of said lists.

This criterion is worth 50 percentage points. All lists shall have an equal allocation of 10 points each. The summary of the result of evaluation using this criterion is presented above.

The Belt

The Belt measures a boxer's pound for pound value by putting premium on the titles he won in different weight divisions. The more championships a boxer wins from different weight classes, the higher his rating goes. Bonus points need to be added, though—boxing supposedly being the model of fairness in sports—to those who (1) were active when there were less divisions, and (2) won their first championships at the higher levels (say, welterweight). The reason for these additional points is basically leveling the field, as it were. Fighters in earlier times could not possibly win as many titles in different weight divisions as they could because fewer divisions then existed. Also, fighters competing at the higher weight divisions could be at a disadvantage because there just are not enough weight classes that are open for them to compete in (unlike a flyweight, for example, for whom 17 weight classes are open to him).

The first bonus point is given to any boxer who was active before the 17 weight divisions got established, a process that started in 1962 (establishment of the WBA). A fighter who was active before 1962, even if he continued to compete beyond that period, like Muhammad Ali, gets the 1 point bonus.

For the second bonus point, extra points are due for boxers who won their first championship belt at higher divisions, viz: Lightweight and Welterweight (.50 point); Super Welterweight, Middleweight, and Super Middleweight (.75 point); Light Heavyweight, Cruiserweight and Heavyweight (1.00 point). Going back to our example, since Ali competed in the heavyweight division, he got a bonus point of 1 point. Adding this to the first bonus point, he got a total bonus point of 2.00.

This criterion is worth 40 percentage points. The summary of the result of evaluation using this criterion is presented below.

The Win

The Win presents stories behind The Belt. It uses four sub-criteria, namely, Career Win Percentages, KO percentages, Quality of Opposition and a measure of how a fighter copes with two intimidation factors—size disadvantage and ring record. The Quality of Opposition has 2 components: one, average win percentages of op-

NAME OF BOXERS	THE BELT (40 %)						SCORING SYSTEM	
	Titles in Different Weight Divisions							
	No.	Bonus	Total	Rank	Score	Points	RANK	SCORE
Sugar Ray Robinson	2	1.50	3.50	9--10	61.37	24.55	1	100.00
Henry Armstrong	3	1.00	4.00	8	68.18	27.27	2	95.45
Muhammad Ali	1	2.00	3.00	11--16	43.18	17.27	3	90.91
Joe Louis	1	2.00	3.00	11--16	43.18	17.27	4	86.36
Roberto Duran	4	0.50	4.50	5--7	77.27	30.91	5	81.82
Willie Pep	1	1.00	2.00	20--22	9.09	3.64	6	77.27
Benny Leonard	1	1.50	2.50	19	18.18	7.27	7	72.73
Jack Johnson	1	2.00	3.00	11--16	43.18	17.27	8	68.18
Jack Dempsey	1	2.00	3.00	11--16	43.18	17.27	9	63.64
Sam Langford	0	2.00	2.00	20--22	9.09	3.64	10	59.09
Billy Conn	1	2.00	3.00	11--16	43.18	17.27	11	54.55
Harry Greb	1	1.75	2.75	17--18	25.00	10.00	12	50.00
Sugar Ray Leonard	4	0.50	4.50	5--7	77.27	30.91	13	45.45
Pernell Whitaker	4	0.50	4.50	5--7	77.27	30.91	14	40.91
Mike Tyson	1	1.00	2.00	20--22	9.09	3.64	15	36.36
Julio Cesar Chavez	3	0.00	3.00	11--16	43.18	17.27	16	31.82
Roy Jones Jr	4	0.75	4.75	4	86.36	34.54	17	27.27
Oscar dela Hoya	6	0.00	6.00	2	95.45	38.18	18	22.73
Shane Mosley	3	0.50	3.50	9--10	61.37	24.55	19	18.18
Bernard Hopkins	2	0.75	2.75	17--18	25.00	10.00	20	13.64
Floyd Mayweather Jr	5	0.00	5.00	3	90.91	36.36	21	9.09
Manny Pacquiao	7	0.00	7.00	1	100.00	40.00	22	4.55

Note: Bonus points are added to those who (1) were active when there were less divisions, and (2) won their first championships at the higher weight classes (say, welterweight).

ponents and, two, a refined view of career win percentages. The second excludes in the evaluation process opponents whose (1) win percentage record is less than 50 percent and (2) total career fights is less than ten (except when the fighter in question is involved in a title fight. An example here would be Ali against Leon Spinks (with the latter having fought for the seventh time only when they met). Thus Spinks ring record would be included in Ali's performance under this sub-criterion. In other words, fighters are rated against fellow fighters with winning properties.

To illustrate: Sam Langford had a total of 315 career fights. But when we exclude his opponents whose career win percentages were less than 50 percent as well as those whose career fights were less than ten, Langford would be left with 177 fights. We then look at how he performed in these 177 fights. We see that he won 100 (out of 177) of these fights. Therefore his rating under this sub-criterion would be 56.5 percent.

There are two intimidation factors: size and ring record. How does a fighter perform against one who significantly outweighs him? And how does

	THE WIN (20%)										
NAME OF BOXERS	Career Win Percentage			KO Percentage			Quality of Opposition				
							Ave Win % of Opponents			Excluded: < 50 win % and <10 bouts		
	%	Rank	Score	%	Rank	Score	%	Rank	Score	%	Rank	Score
Sugar Ray Robinson	86.50	15	36.36	63.01	15	36.36	66.94	14	40.91	83.65	14	40.91
Henry Armstrong	82.78	19	18.18	67.79	11	54.55	63.02	15	36.36	82.84	16	31.82
Muhammad Ali	91.80	5	81.82	66.07	12	50.00	82.46	2	95.45	94.92	3	90.91
Joe Louis	95.65	2	95.45	78.79	4	86.36	74.62	9	63.64	95.31	2	95.45
Roberto Duran	86.55	14	40.91	67.96	10	59.09	70.19	12	50.00	80.72	18	22.73
Willie Pep	95.02	3	90.91	30.57	20	13.64	56.76	19	18.18	92.90	4	86.36
Benny Leonard	84.33	17	27.27	38.25	19	18.18	51.96	22	4.55	83.33	15	36.36
Jack Johnson	72.28	21	9.09	54.79	17	27.27	58.76	18	22.73	69.64	21	9.09
Jack Dempsey	79.52	20	13.64	77.27	5	81.82	54.37	21	9.09	71.43	20	13.64
Sam Langford	64.44	22	4.55	63.05	14	40.91	56.60	20	13.64	56.50	22	4.55
Billy Conn	83.12	18	22.73	23.44	21	9.09	61.06	17	27.27	84.78	11	54.55
Harry Greb	86.96	11--12	52.22	18.46	22	4.55	61.85	16	31.82	87.50	8	68.18
Sugar Ray Leonard	90.00	8	68.18	69.44	9	63.64	82.26	3	90.91	89.47	7	72.73
Pernell Whitaker	86.96	11--12	52.22	42.50	18	22.73	78.25	7	72.73	84.62	12	50.00
Mike Tyson	86.21	16	31.82	88.00	1	100.00	81.45	4	86.36	84.00	13	45.45
Julio Cesar Chavez	93.04	4	86.36	80.37	3	90.91	69.86	13	45.45	78.38	19	18.18
Roy Jones Jr	91.53	6	77.27	74.07	8	68.18	80.83	5	81.82	90.38	6	77.27
Oscar dela Hoya	86.67	13	45.45	76.92	6	77.27	88.03	1	100.00	86.36	9	63.64
Shane Mosley	88.46	9	63.64	84.78	2	95.45	72.32	10	59.09	85.37	10	59.09
Bernard Hopkins	87.50	10	59.09	65.31	13	45.45	75.78	8	68.18	82.50	17	27.27
Floyd Mayweather Jr	100.00	1	100.00	62.50	16	31.82	79.08	6	77.27	100.00	1	100.00
Manny Pacquiao	90.91	7	72.73	76.00	7	72.73	71.85	11	54.55	92.11	5	81.82

NAME OF BOXERS	THE WIN (20%), continuation							SCORING SYSTEM	
	Intimidation Factors								
	Size (10 lbs up)			Ring Record (90% up)			Ave Score	Points (20%)		
	%	Rank	Score	%	Rank	Score			RANK	SCORE
Sugar Ray Robinson	78.30	14	40.91	58.33	17	27.27	37.12	7.42	1	100.00
Henry Armstrong	83.33	12	50.00	80.00	10	59.09	41.67	8.33	2	95.45
Muhammad Ali	100.00	1--8	84.09	89.47	4	86.36	81.44	16.29	3	90.91
Joe Louis	100.00	1--8	84.09	83.33	9	63.64	81.44	16.29	4	86.36
Roberto Duran	70.59	18	22.73	47.06	19	18.18	35.61	7.12	5	81.82
Willie Pep	100.00	1--8	84.09	66.67	14--15	38.64	55.30	11.06	6	77.27
Benny Leonard	89.47	10	59.09	0.00	22	4.55	25.00	5.00	7	72.73
Jack Johnson	75.00	16	31.82	100.00	1--2	97.73	32.96	6.59	8	68.18
Jack Dempsey	100.00	1--8	84.09	57.14	18	22.73	37.50	7.50	9	63.64
Sam Langford	44.44	21	9.09	40.00	21	9.09	13.64	2.73	10	59.09
Billy Conn	77.78	15	36.36	60.00	16	31.82	30.30	6.06	11	54.55
Harry Greb	85.71	11	54.55	41.67	20	13.64	37.49	7.50	12	50.00
Sugar Ray Leonard	100.00	1--8	84.09	76.92	11--12	52.28	71.97	14.39	13	45.45
Pernell Whitaker	73.33	17	27.27	76.92	11--12	52.28	46.21	9.24	14	40.91
Mike Tyson	69.23	20	13.64	84.62	8	68.18	57.58	11.52	15	36.36
Julio Cesar Chavez	90.00	9	63.65	88.46	5	81.82	64.40	12.88	16	31.82
Roy Jones Jr	81.48	13	45.45	87.50	7	72.73	70.45	14.09	17	27.27
Oscar dela Hoya	100.00	1--8	84.09	73.91	13	45.45	69.32	13.86	18	22.73
Shane Mosley	70.00	19	18.18	66.67	14--15	38.64	55.68	11.14	19	18.18
Bernard Hopkins	40.00	22	4.55	88.24	6	77.27	46.97	9.39	20	13.64
Floyd Mayweather Jr	100.00	1--8	84.09	100.00	1--2	97.73	81.82	16.36	21	9.09
Manny Pacquiao	100.00	1--8	84.09	90.48	3	90.91	76.14	15.23	22	4.55

he perform against one who has a reputation of winning fights on a more or less consistent basis? These questions are what this sub-criterion intends to address.

The question of size marks the fighting weight of a fighter at 25 years of age, which is widely assumed to be the normal age at which male human beings stop growing—physically, that is. Such an assumption can be debated on, but this book did not make it up; it is based on the prevailing scientific view that relates to the study of human growth, particularly among males.

The current rating process applies this sub-criterion in this manner: The weight of Boxer A at age 25 is a given. If a boxer fought as featherweight, for example, when he was 25 years old, the normal fighting weight of Boxer A is assumed to be 126 pounds. The win percentage of Boxer A from his fights that involved opponents who weighed more than 126 pounds by at least 10 pounds, regardless of the weight division at which they contested, is then computed.

Let us take Manny Pacquiao as an example. He was a featherweight (126 pounds) when he turned 25. This sub-criterion assumes that, by nature, 126 pounds would be Pacquiao's fighting weight. Thus all boxers he faced who weighed more than 136 pounds would be considered intimidating, from his perspective. In all, he has so far fought 4 opponents that weighed more than 136 pounds—De La Hoya, Hatton, Cotto, and Clottey. Since he has beaten all 4 opponents, Pacquiao's rating under this sub-criterion would be 100 percent.

The ring record sub-criterion works similarly. The only difference is that instead of looking at the weights, the win-loss performance of opponents becomes the variable input. The win percentage of Boxer A from his fights that involved opponents who had a winning record of at least 90 percent (in at least 25 fights) is then derived.

Let us now take Oscar De La Hoya as an example. He fought a total of 23 elite boxers who had career win percentages of at least 90 percent at the time of their match-up. He won 17 times in these 23 battles. He thus earns a rating of 73.9 percent under this sub-category.

In sum, The Belt and The Win further sieve the rankings of the world's greatest boxers of all time, according to the first criterion, The List. This criterion is worth 20 percentage points.

SUMMARY OF RATINGS

NAME OF BOXERS	THE LIST (40%)	THE BELT (40%)	THE WIN (20%)	TOTAL POINTS	OVERALL RANK
Sugar Ray Robinson	32.00	24.55	7.27	63.82	2
Henry Armstrong	26.88	27.27	8.33	62.48	4
Muhammad Ali	29.48	17.27	16.36	63.11	3
Joe Louis	24.64	17.27	16.36	58.27	8
Roberto Duran	20.85	30.91	7.12	58.88	7
Willie Pep	22.39	3.64	11.06	37.09	15
Benny Leonard	16.67	7.27	4.85	28.79	19
Jack Johnson	6.82	17.27	6.36	30.45	17
Jack Dempsey	14.09	17.27	7.42	38.79	14
Sam Langford	5.91	3.64	2.73	12.27	22
Billy Conn	6.36	17.27	5.91	29.55	18
Harry Greb	13.18	10.00	7.35	30.53	16
Sugar Ray Leonard	6.36	30.91	14.47	51.74	10
Pernell Whitaker	5.91	30.91	9.39	46.21	11
Mike Tyson	6.82	3.64	11.67	22.12	21
Julio Cesar Chavez	9.55	17.27	12.88	39.70	13
Roy Jones Jr	9.55	34.54	14.09	58.18	9
Oscar dela Hoya	7.96	38.18	13.94	60.07	6
Shane Mosley	7.96	24.55	11.21	43.72	12
Bernard Hopkins	7.96	10.00	9.55	27.50	20
Floyd Mayweather Jr	9.55	36.36	16.36	62.27	5
Manny Pacquiao	14.00	40.00	15.30	69.30	1

The resulting points summary is presented on Pages 90 and 91.

Rank-Based Points System

Having set the criteria for rating and their relative weights, the rating process proceeds with application of a point system, based on ranking.

All boxers are ranked on the basis of their performances (fight records) under each criterion. A corresponding score, equitably distributed among the 22 fighters, is assigned to each rank. The relative weight of each criterion is then applied to the score, and the resulting points generated from all criteria are summed up to derive the total scores credited to each fighter.

NOTES ON THE RATINGS
The List

Since each boxer was already ranked in each of the four lists, what was left was to apply the corresponding scores. A fighter who was not part of a list (say The Ring) but present in another list (say ESPN) got zero score in the first; however, he got the ranked-based score in the second. In the case of the pound for pound list, we first applied the ranking process before assigning the scores. Basis for the ranking was the number of years a fighter had been named by The Ring as pound for pound champion (ie, a fighter who had been named twice would be ahead of those who had been name only once). The total scores were then derived and multiplied by the weight assigned to the criterion, which is 50 percent.

A question maybe raised as to why Robinson, among others, got zero points for the pound for pound list. This, admittedly, was a weak part of the ranking process. The Ring started to publish its annual pound for pound list only in 1989, which in effect left out those who competed prior to that period even if the likes of Robinson and Armstrong would concededly be hands down choices for such a pound for pound list.

To somehow compensate for this, the book used 4 lists (out of five) that included in their rankings fighters who competed in an era as early as the 1900s.

The Belt

Manny Pacquiao's 7 titles in 7 weight divisions have propelled him to the top of the rankings under this category. De La Hoya's 6 titles came in second, while Mayweather and Roy Jones came in tied for 3rd and 4th places with their 5 titles apiece.

A footnote here may be necessary with respect to Pacquiao's 7 titles. One of the 7, at featherweight, was not awarded by any of the existing sanctioning bodies, but by the Ring Magazine. This happened after he defeated Marco Antonio Barrera in 2003 who, at the time, was considered the "People's Champ." Prior to their encounter, Barrera had defeated erstwhile undefeated and elite fighters in the featherweight division, notably Prince Naseem Hamed, Erik Morales and Johnny Tapia. Beyond that, this book is not competent to defend the competence of The Ring to award such a recognition to a fighter.

The Win

Floyd Mayweather topped all boxers in the career win percentage category, having a 40-0 win-loss record. The top placers in the 3 lists, notably Sugar Ray Robinson (at number 15), Benny Leonard (no. 17), and Henry Armstrong (no 19) had a weak showing in this category.

Under the KO percentage category, Mike Tyson out punched all of them. Again, the top listers took a beating here. Robinson managed to land at number 15, but Leonard (no. 19) and Pep (no. 20) had to settle somewhere at the tail end.

For the Quality of Opposition sub-criterion, Mayweather, again, topped this category. Robinson, Armstrong, Pep and Benny Leonard comprised the bottom half of the ranking.

For the Intimidation Factor (size) sub-criterion, 6 fighters tied for the first to sixth places under this category. Again, Robinson and the rest of the top listers had to settle at the lower end of the pack.

For the Ring Record sub-criterion, Mayweather once more topped this category. Duran, Greb, Langford and Leonard—in that order—took the last four places.

SUMMARY OF RATINGS

In summary, Manny Pacquiao garnered the highest total points of 69.30. He got most of his points from The Belt, who topped this category, followed by Oscar De La Hoya. Sugar Ray Robinson came in second with 63.82. Muhammad Ali follows at third with 63.11. The other top two placers in the three lists, namely Armstrong and Duran, came in 4th and 7th, respectively.

Summary of ratings using the 3 criteria is presented on Page 92.

In essence, this book differs from the four lists in how it puts Sugar Ray Robinson at the standings. From number one, he slid down to number 2. Manny Pacquiao took his place at the top. Also, Floyd Mayweather came in strong at fifth, trailing Ali at third and Armstrong at fourth.

Robinson and, to a lesser extent, Armstrong, hardly showed up in the The Win category.

It is in the context of applying the totality of the above criteria—particularly The Belt and The Win—that Pacquiao has established himself as a cut above the rest, without equal, and clearly greater than Sugar Ray Robinson, Henry Armstrong, and Muhammad Ali, among others.

At this point, it may help to refresh the data from The Win criterion. For example, 41 of Robinson's 200 fights were against opponents whose average career win percentage was less than 50 percent. In fights where these low-quality opponents were excluded, Robinson's winning rate goes down to 83.65, compared to his career win rate of 86.50. This pales in comparison to the resume of Pacquiao's opponents. Pacquiao has an average of 87 percent winning rate against high-quality opponents, compared to his career winning rate of 91 percent.

Even after Robinson had collected world crowns in the Welterweight and Middleweight divisions and after having compiled a ring record of 127-1-2 win-loss-draw record in 130 professional fights, he still fought opponents with dubious ring records—those with either ring experiences of less than 10 fights or winning rates of less than 50 percent.

Thus one could even argue that Pacquiao's sparring partners (some of whom were either title holders or former world champions) have fight records that were superior to that of many of Robinson's opponents. And Pacquiao goes through at least 130 rounds of sparring sessions to prepare for his big fights.

Altogether—that is, including low-quality opponents—the average career win percentage of Robinson's opponents was 67, compared to Pacquiao's 72 percent.

With respect to the rest of the greatest fighters, the quality of their opposition was simply inferior in relation to those of Pacquiao, Mayweather, De

La Hoya and the rest who figured prominently atop the rankings presented in this book.

By way of concluding the process of ranking the world's greatest fighters, this book has to admit some deficiencies. Something had to be missed in the foregoing analyses. Pacquiao and most of the elite fighters of this era (except probably Roberto Duran) have yet to show the kind of longevity—or staying power—that Robinson had shown in boxing. Robinson remained active inside the ring (not only as referee but a competitor) until his early 50s.

At such an advanced age when other legends had decided to hang up their gloves, Robinson continued to compete at a high level (read: fighting not only for himself but for the fans as well). While indicative of his passion for the sport (others who continued to fight when they should have had retired did so for want of money), this also negatively affected his winning rate. It pulled down his overall rating.

Here, anyone can feel free to speculate: If Pacquiao, Mayweather and the rest of today's top-level fighters continue to fight the way Robinson and Duran did, would their fight records look impeccable as they are today? We don't

REVIEW OF RANKINGS BY CRITERION

THE LIST		THE BELT		THE WIN		OVERALL RANK AND	TOTAL
RANK AND NAME	POINTS	RANK AND NAME	POINTS	RANK AND NAME	POINTS	NAME	POINTS
1 Sugar Ray Robinson	32.00	1 Manny Pacquiao	40.00	1 Muhammad Ali	16.36	1 Manny Pacquiao	69.30
2 Muhammad Ali	29.48	2 Oscar De La Hoya	38.18	2 Floyd Mayweather	16.36	2 Sugar Ray Robinson	63.82
3 Henry Armstrong	26.88	3 Floyd Mayweather	36.36	3 Joe Louis	16.36	3 Muhammad Ali	63.11
4 Joe Louis	24.64	4 Roy Jones Jr	34.54	4 Manny Pacquiao	15.30	4 Henry Armstrong	62.48
5 Willie Pep	22.39	5 Pernell Whitaker	30.91	5 Sugar Ray Leonard	14.47	5 Floyd Mayweather Jr	62.27
6 Roberto Duran	20.85	6 Roberto Duran	30.91	6 Roy Jones Jr	14.09	6 Oscar dela Hoya	60.07
7 Benny Leonard	16.67	7 Sugar Ray Leonard	30.91	7 Oscar dela Hoya	13.94	7 Roberto Duran	58.88
8 Jack Dempsey	14.09	8 Henry Armstrong	27.27	8 Julio Cesar Chavez	12.88	8 Joe Louis	58.27
9 Harry Greb	14.00	9 Shane Mosley	24.55	9 Mike Tyson	11.67	9 Roy Jones Jr	58.18
10 Floyd Mayweather	13.18	10 Sugar Ray Robinson	24.55	10 Shane Mosley	11.21	10 Sugar Ray Leonard	51.74
11 Julio Cesar Chavez	9.55	11 Billy Conn	17.27	11 Willie Pep	11.06	11 Pernell Whitaker	46.21
12 Roy Jones Jr	9.55	12 Jack Dempsey	17.27	12 Bernard Hopkins	9.55	12 Shane Mosley	43.72
13 Bernard Hopkins	9.55	13 Jack Johnson	17.27	13 Pernell Whitaker	9.39	13 Julio Cesar Chavez	39.70
14 Manny Pacquiao	7.96	14 Joe Louis	17.27	14 Henry Armstrong	8.33	14 Jack Dempsey	38.79
15 Oscar dela Hoya	7.96	15 Julio Cesar Chavez	17.27	15 Jack Dempsey	7.42	15 Willie Pep	37.09
16 Shane Mosley	7.96	16 Muhammad Ali	17.27	16 Harry Greb	7.35	16 Harry Greb	30.53
17 Mike Tyson	6.82	17 Bernard Hopkins	10.00	17 Sugar Ray Robinson	7.27	17 Jack Johnson	30.45
18 Jack Johnson	6.82	18 Harry Greb	10.00	18 Roberto Duran	7.12	18 Billy Conn	29.55
19 Billy Conn	6.36	19 Benny Leonard	7.27	19 Jack Johnson	6.36	19 Benny Leonard	28.79
20 Sugar Ray Leonard	6.36	20 Mike Tyson	3.64	20 Billy Conn	5.91	20 Bernard Hopkins	27.50
21 Pernell Whitaker	5.91	21 Sam Langford	3.64	21 Benny Leonard	4.85	21 Mike Tyson	22.12
22 Sam Langford	5.91	22 Willie Pep	3.64	22 Sam Langford	2.73	22 Sam Langford	12.27

know. And we guess nobody does.

This book's current rankings imply several things. One, they can change anytime, depending on how the boxers who are still active at present are performing. If they lose, they take themselves out of the leader board. If they win, their standing will be affirmed and further established. Two, they serve to reinforce the reasons why Pacquiao, Robinson, De La Hoya and Dempsey, were the most-watched fighters in boxing history. And three, the debate on who is the greatest boxer of all time, pound for pound, is far from closed.

On the basis of the foregoing analysis, this book finds that Manny Pacquiao is boxing's GOAT (greatest of all time). His win over Puerto Rico's Miguel Cotto on November 14, 2009 at Las Vegas, Nevada, USA, further established his statistical superiority (he already got the highest point even before he beat Cotto with 6 world titles and sharing the top spot of The Belt criterion with Oscar De La Hoya).

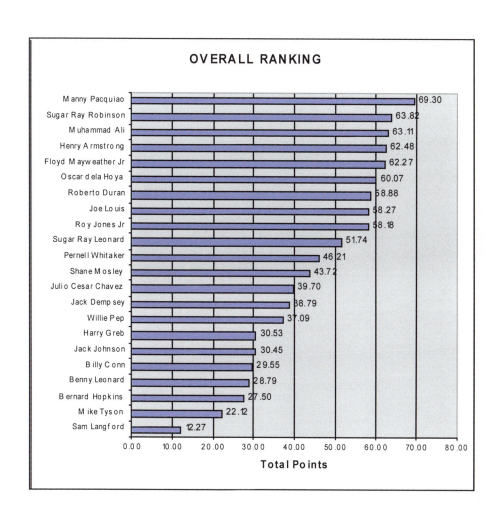

Part Four: The Legend Grows

In a profound way, what the failed Pacquiao-Mayweather negotiations meant was Pacquiao's dashing the notion that he could stand his ground only in the ring. He showed that he also had what it took to deserve respect outside of the ring. He could break down situations and he had enough courage to stand by what he thought was right.

When the Mayweathers accused Pacquiao of using an esoteric drug or "A-side Meth" and demanded random blood testing when nobody knew how blood samples could be tested for such a magical drug, Pacquiao knew that—one, the Mayweathers wanted him psychologically battered even before the bell could ring in the event a fight with him would happen and, two, failing to snare him in a mind-game, they had to look for a way out of the fight.

What the likes of Mayweather refused to give Pacquiao credit for was his convictions—and his capacity to make informed choices in support of them. Pacquiao's first American promoter, Murad Muhammad, often referred to Pacquiao as "the kid." Early in Pacquiao's career, people in dark suits often thought he lived by what others whispered to him; they underestimated his ability to comprehend on his own the kind of information that is not solely tied to boxing gloves.

When Pacquiao brought Murad to court for misconduct, he braved an environment that dramatized the inconsequence of those who sweat it out to make a living in relation to the awesome presence of the powerful. But he showed that he had full control of his facts, and went on to win an out-of-court settlement with Murad.

Still on the failed negotiations with Mayweather, Arum has quoted Pacquiao as saying that "I am a Filipino. I cannot be bullied inside and outside the ring."

On March 4, 2010, some members of Philippine media covering a press conference in Los Angeles, USA, that was meant to promote the May 1 Floyd Mayweather Jr-Shane Mosley, felt bullied when they were barred from interviewing Mayweather.

FOR FILIPINOS WHOSE LEADERS throughout history have had little to show in terms of advancing the country's interests in forging international treaties or agreements, Pacquiao's off-ring exploits come around like a whiff of fresh air.

In a context where millions of his compatriots work as virtual slaves in other countries, Pacquiao has managed to highlight how far he has gone. He not only issues paychecks to clients and employees of other nationalities, he pays them in a way that makes them proud to be associated with a Filipino. Moreover, and in a more profound sense, many Filipinos overseas have felt having been accorded with a new-found respect from the rest of the world by virtue of sharing Manny's nationality.

Manny Pacquiao meets former US President Bill Clinton in Las Vegas, USA. **Photo by Google Images.**

And it's not only about nationality. Without saying anything, Pacquiao has been eloquent about the value of nationalism. For instance, unlike most big-time global athletes and celebrities who earned most of their incomes in the US and transferred their domiciles to the US to save millions of dollars from tax payments, Pacquiao has chosen to stay in the Philippines.

He has in fact fortified his citizenship. During the 2010 Philippine elections, he ran for and won a congressional seat, representing the Province of Sarangani.

Flashing scenes from Manny "The Pacman" Pacquiao the boxer to Emmanuel D. Pacquiao the politician is one more glitter to a story that has captivated millions.

For the majority of his countrymen who continue to wallow in poverty, Pacquiao represents hope. For those who grope in the darkness of doubt, he is like the flicker that assures them of their capacity to succeed.

The man who had nothing early in life has now almost everything. He has money and all it can buy. With an estimated asset of close to 70 million dollars, he is number six in Forbe's list of the world's wealthiest athletes. He has a multitude of fans. He is famous. He has graced the cover of Time Magazine and Readers' Digest. He has appeared in mainstream American TV talk shows. Hollywood celebrities have called on him. Former US Presidents Bill Clinton and George Bush had went out of their way to acknowledge him.

In a relatively so short a time, the Pacquiao legend has grown. And his celebrity status continues to soar.

Manny Pacquiao finds it necessary to connect to **His God** every time a job needs to be done. **Photo by Photobucket.com**

CRUSADER IN THE RING

Already a boxing icon and a political leader—and yet there is something more in being Manny Pacquiao.

With Cotto and Clottey—both top-level welterweights—out of the way, it is time to contemplate the miracle that Pacquiao is, as Al Bernstein suggested. And as the Mayweathers have alleged about Pacman's benefiting from either PEDs or magical potions, let's delve on the intangibles of human (or superhuman, if you may) achievement.

In each of Pacman's fights, there's one usual sight that provides contrast to the boisterous atmosphere of the boxing arena. It is a sight of humility. It is almost an expression of inner peace. The boxer makes a sign of the cross and marks himself as disciple of the Roman Catholic faith. The gesture not only affirms one's faith in His God—that the Lord is with him every step of his way ("Emmanuel" means "God is with us"); it also acknowledges one's inconsequence before God; that he is a creation of no one (not even by the multitude who cheers for him inside a Las Vegas boxing venue) but by Him. The meaning of The Pacman's gesture resonates, and his being human shines through even more when he says "*I pray to God that no one will get hurt.*"

As a footnote, though, one may find madness in all of this if He was God. Why would people adore boxing in the first place if it risks the health of boxers? It is a question that demands answers, but one that may have to be addressed by another story. It resembles a question about the madness of war among countries, although this, too, is another story.

Turning back to Pacquiao, we find that as he enters the boxing ring before a fight, he searches his own corner and, upon finding it, kneels down in prayer. He does the same after the fight. He repeatedly makes the sign of the cross before, during and after each bout, sometimes during each round. Outside of the ring, his humble disposition makes it easy for the uninitiated to take his side.

Without an army, The Pacman is a Crusader. Both inside and outside the ring, he is a celebrity endorser of Catholicism. He is an untitled ambassador to the world—for present and future generations—from the Vatican.

> *Has any fighter ever rendered more excitement, more stimulation and more enthusiasm for his job than **Pacman** has since he made his HBO debut on June 23, 2001 in Las Vegas against South Africa's **Lehlohonolo Ledwaba**?*
>
> *No, the greatest fighter fighting the toughest opposition in HBO's brief ring history (dating back to **Mike Weaver-Larry Holmes** in 1979) and producing the brightest sparks has been **Pacquiao**.*
>   --**Michael Marley**, Examiner.com

WHO CAN STOP THE PACMAN?

Given his recent successes inside the ring, the question that is often raised is not what else he can accomplish. The question scans the horizon if ever there is a force on earth that can stop The Pacman.

Two possible answers. First, not only are people lining up to fight Pacquiao for the money (big pay goes to whoever is in front of him), they also look forward to relishing the honor of being the one to have stopped the Pacquiao juggernaut. Thus enormous material and psychic rewards await would-be Pacquiao opponents. Just the same, however, many boxing fans still believe that only a few active fighters today in Pacquiao's weight class are capable of posing any serious threat to his dominance at the top. In this scant list can be mentioned the names of Floyd Mayweather Jr, Amir Khan and those who rule the higher divisions, like Sergio Martinez and Paul Williams.

Second, even the best of them fade to the sunset. Changes in psychological make up, not to mention physical wear and tear, can debase anybody's desire to win.

In all his boxing life, Pacquiao has leaned on his prayers for self-assurance and self-confidence. Problem is, even stories of success have hints of underlying limitations. The more successful one becomes, he or she might no longer feel the need for self-assurance. What one has become is the assurance. He or she believes he already has enough power to get things done. Old ways get lost in the scheme of things and, in Manny's case, he can very well stop being superstitious, or cease praying the way he used to—that is, praying like everything has depended on His God.

If that happens, new ways of looking at things can affect his bio-rhythm, the pulse rate, the drive, the focus, etc. either in a positive or negative manner. When the next bell rings, will his fighting heart switch itself on like it always did before? If the overall flow of his bio-rhythm works differently like it used to, he is bound to make mistakes inside the ring. His motor apparatus can fail. Being slow in reflexes is a sure recipe for disaster in bouts contested at such a high level where he competes. A moment of weakness can be fatal; and he does not need a top-notch opponent to lose a fight. The Pacman can stop The Pacman.

Finally, there is one mighty opponent nobody can outlast—time. The greatest boxers may have tried to beat this adversary; none of them succeeded.

In his youth, Sugar Ray Robinson lost only once in his first 132 fights. After competing for 11 years at age 30, he lost 18 of his succeeding 68 matches.

Roberto Duran lost only once in his first 73 fights. But starting at age 29, he lost 15 of his next 46 bouts. And at age 43, he lost 7 of his final 18 fights.

Julio Cesar Chavez was undefeated in his first 90 fights. But after he turned 32 and being active for 14 straight years, he lost 6 of his next 25 fights.

Oscar De La Hoya never lost until his 32nd fight, at age 26. From age 30 onwards, he lost 4 of his next 7 bouts.

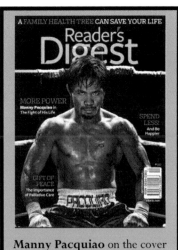

Manny Pacquiao on the cover of the Reader's Digest, Asia Edition. **Photo by Google Images.**

The examples can go on and on. But the message of each story is the same: nobody beats time. Old age may not be a curse. But like all properties of nature, it needs to be managed. Many legends were found wanting not because of lack of skill or physical fitness. Rather, they embarrassed themselves for not knowing when to retire.

Manny Pacquiao will soon turn 32. And the legends like him have shown wear and tear at this point of their respective careers. He has shown none of it in his last 6—even 7—fights. But sooner or later something will have to give. If time—or age—had stopped the best of athletes, it could stop the Pacman, too. As to when it happens, however, only time can tell. Not a few well-meaning friends, like his Chief Trainer Freddie Roach, have in fact advised him to plan his exit while he is on top.

What can make retiring an easy decision for Pacquiao to do is the secure and solid standing he has established for himself in the sport. Excepting hecklers and those who just can't leave so much money on the table (which may not necessarily be wrong), many people think there really is nothing left to prove himself.

In the meantime, boxing fans can feel lucky for having shared in real time this era with Manny Pacquiao—a man of boundless faith and courage, a rare athletic find, the world's greatest pound-for-pound fighter of all time.

CPSIA information can be obtained
at www.ICGtesting.com
Printed in the USA
LVIC04n2016301113
363371LV00013B/162